Inspirational Hymn and Song Stories
of the Twentieth Century

AMBASSADOR

BELFAST, NORTHERN IRELAND
GREENVILLE, USA

Inspirational Hymn and Song Stories of the Twentieth Century

by
PAUL DAVIS

Introduction by Marijohn Wilkin
Foreword by Jessy Dixon

AMBASSADOR
BELFAST, NORTHERN IRELAND
GREENVILLE, USA

Inspirational Hymn and Song Stories of the Twentieth Century
© Copyright 2001 Paul Davis

ISBN 1 84030 101 5

Ambassador Publications
a division of
Ambassador Productions Ltd.
Providence House
Ardenlee Street,
Belfast,
BT6 8QJ
Northern Ireland
www.ambassador-productions.com

Emerald House
427 Wade Hampton Blvd.
Greenville
SC 29609, USA
www.emeraldhouse.com

This keepsake book is ideal for the pastor, preacher, teacher, student, layperson, music fan, the Christian reader and the casual reader.

From worldwide sources, these songs were heavily recorded and published throughout the last Century. They include chart successes, movie hits, modern hymns & contemporary choruses.

Each inspirational song-story is preceded by an appropriate KJV Bible text and songs, scriptures and song-writers are listed alphabetically.

Hymn and Song Stories

 Dedicated to

My Dear Wife -
Hazel

Our Wonderful Children & Grandchildren -
Anita & Ed McGirr
(& Nathanael and Rachel)
Laura & Paul Ewers
Wes & Sue Davis

Our Faithful Parents -
Helen & Tom Davis
Rose & Walter Scott

Our Loving Church -
Leighton Christian Fellowship, England
and Worldwide

All Our Friends -
In The World Of Music

Acknowledgments

Pat and Dave Bilbrough
Bryn & Sally Haworth
Jim and Judy Leigh,
Debbie and Harley Rollins
Bill Gaither
Jerry Arhelger
Anne and Cliff Barrows
Miriam and James Blackwood
Francine and Cecil Blackwood
Sir Cliff Richard, OBE
Karlene and George Beverly Shea
Adelaide and George Hamilton IV
Joy and Samuel Purdy
Jessy Dixon
Marijohn Wilkin
John Pantry
Chris Bowater
Robert Lamont
John Nice
Bob Gillman
Roger Hill
Samuel Lowry
Laura Ewers
and Hazel Davis

 **Foreword** *by Jessy Dixon*

I agree with the great founder of the Salvation Army-General William Booth(1829-1912)-when he said, *"Music is for the soul what wind is for the ship, blowing her onwards in the direction in which she is steered!"* Throughout the history of Old Testament and New Testament times including up to this day, singing has always played a prominent part in the worship and daily life of God's people, whether they lived BC or AD.

The first song in the Bible was sung by Lamech in the book of Genesis and it was not uncommon for the Jews to compose a song celebrating some special victory or religious experience such as the Red Sea crossing of Exodus 15. The book of Psalms has been designated "The Song Book of Israel," and it contains many varieties of songs covering many experiences. In his epistles, the Apostle Paul urges us believers to sing and in the Book of Revelation, the Apostle John speaks often of heavenly singing.

It's important that our Christian testimony in song comes from lives truly regenerated by God's grace. I readily admit that for many years I was a gospel singer who did not know in personal experience the God of whom I sang. This left me with a feeling of frustration, disenchanted with my career. Although I was outwardly highly successful, I was inwardly empty. I praise God that I came to realise that there had to be more than that! I needed to commit my body, soul and spirit to Him and His Song. I needed to know the Lord personally and be committed to His Cause.

I thank God for the friend who invited me to a Salvation Seminar meeting where I heard the minister preach the gospel. I realised the necessity of personal commitment to Christ was what I was looking for to give me complete fulfilment in the joy of singing gospel music! Next morning in my car, I heard a preacher preaching the same message on the radio. I knew that was more than coincidence - God was speaking to me! So I invited the Lord into my life and made my commitment, there and then!

The change of heart gave me a change of attitude in my gospel music career. Now I have a reason to sing because I know Whom I am singing about! It's a privilege to get to know the great unknowable God in the person of Jesus Christ.

I am so glad that my friend, Paul Davis, has put pen to paper and documented these exciting song stories. The impact of each well-known song becomes stronger when one gets to know how each song was written and the way God inspired its writer.

Thank you, Paul, for a very faith-inspiring publication. My hope is that very soon I will be blessed by being able to read a second volume!

Jessy Dixon
Chicago, Illinois, USA

Introduction *by Marijohn Wilkin*

The celebrated German reformationist-Martin Luther (1483-1546) was a monk and theologian who led the Protestant Reformation and translated the Bible into the German language. He declared that *"next to the Word of God, music deserves the Highest Praise! The Gift of Language combined with the Gift of Song was given to man that he should proclaim the Word of God through music."*

No one better understands that powerful quotation better than my friend, Paul Davis-the author of this book. It was through his unquestioned love of gospel music that we first met in London when my song-"One Day At A Time" was first introduced there, long before it became a hit.

I will never forget Paul's gentle spirit while he interviewed me. He displayed a sincerity and genuine interest in not only "One Day At A Time" but all my music.

Most sincerely, I count it an honour to be in this inspirational book of Twentieth Century songwriters. I am convinced that you-the reader-will be inspired by the wonderful stories and fascinating people behind these distinguished gospel songs!

Marijohn Wilkin,
Nashville, Tennessee, USA

Alphabetical Hymn and Song Index

Introduction by Marijohn Wilkin
Foreword by Jessy Dixon

 **Prologue**

More than any Century before it, the Twentieth Century was rich in diverse genres of Christian music. Local "calls to worship" in the new church culture of that new Century nearly always meant congregations joining together in "singing the gospel". Initially, musical accompaniment was generally quite simple. What mattered was down-to-earth sincerity and heart-felt identification with the sentiments of the songs from the performers. That flavoured the genres with genuine emotion- later called "soul". Where worship was a joy rather than a duty, harmony singing prospered, sometimes backed by traditional stringed instruments such as auto-harp and guitar. But more usually, piano or harmonium and later electric guitars and percussion were used. From generation to generation, gospel songs and hymns were lovingly handed down through church community traditions.

The hard-working, Victorian pioneers of the Industrial and Agricultural Revolutions doggedly settled into a new religious culture as they adventurously sought social and economic progression amid much hardship. To ease the pain of their deep struggles and dire deprivations, they would often take to singing songs of inspiration. The front parlour's piano or organ became the family gathering place.

To the accompaniment of a family member, they loved to enjoy, testify and sing about their faith. Throughout the previous Century, ever-expanding evangelistic campaigns and revivals spawned new spiritual life as churches and tabernacles sprouted up everywhere. It was not long before each church community would develop its own particular style of what they called "music ministry". Choirs, quartets and soloists sprang up, blossomed and flourished. Where ecclesiastical buildings were not available, itinerant ministers and musicians carried the gospel into the countryside and urban environs.

The spiritual revivals of the Nineteenth Century opened the way for a new form of Christian musical expression in the next Century. Isaac Watts, several generations before, conformed to familiar metrical schemes namely long, short, and common - for tunes already known. Then the likes of the Eighteenth Century's Charles Wesley wrote regardless of any known tunes or conventions. The enthusiastic, new converts to Christianity from Victorian days were common people of the working class, keen to introduce familiar, singable melodies into their worship. Composers before that time, writing for the church, tended to be "educated" musicians from the establishment. A new genre of home-grown writer and singer was to spring up as a result of the Victorian revivals. Their emphasis became the creation of more folksy singable types of Christian song. The evangelicals and puritans being democratic and 'of the people' in philosophy, embraced these radical changes with some enthusiasm. As evangelical denominations became more and more accepted by the establishment, the further use of popular tunes was extended. The newly converted common people within a generation succeeded in introducing spirituality into their every-day poetry and music. A very important event in the on-going evolution of Christian music expansion was the publication in 1873 by singer/songwriter, Ira Sankey of his "Sacred Songs and Solos" book. Well into the Twentieth Century, it sold in millions as he popularised hymns and gospel songs on both sides of the Atlantic. By the turn of the Twentieth Century, history documents that this musical movement helped Christianity to move nearer to the soul of the common people.

Folk style rhyme and music successfully blended into the cosmopolitan character of all denominations. By the end of the

Nineteenth Century, gospel music was emotionally and culturally having an impact as never before on individuals and even upon society as a whole. Even the great popular composers of the secular field (such as Arthur Sullivan of Gilbert & Sullivan fame) were contributing to the blossoming field of popular hymnody. Great gospel personalities started to emerge, two of the greatest spanned the end of the Nineteenth century and the start of the Twentieth century. Fanny Crosby was to epitomise the best of the newly evolving gospel songwriters and Ira Sankey was to fulfil the same role as a gospel music performer.

More than any other songwriter, Fanny Crosby captured the attention of millions with her simple yet meaningful gospel songs. She devoted her long, fruitful life to transposing the great spiritual truths of the Christian faith into singable rhyme and melody. Fully persuaded of those truths, her life enjoyed and radiated "Blessed Assurance" (to quote her famous song). Ira Sankey gave birth to many vocalising-successors in the Twentieth Century. The subsequent decades saw many performers successfully fulfil their gospel-singing or song-leading ministries initially in the mass evangelism arena. This *gospel music train* included Charles Alexander, Homer Rodeheaver, Gypsy Smith, Cliff Barrows and George Beverly Shea.

As leisure time increased, the *gospel music train* in the second half of the Twentieth Century was to usher in the arrival of contemporary Christian music in the entertainment sphere. Many artistes expanded the genre to daringly embrace the risky new idea of Christian music entertainment. This relatively new entertainment phenomenon from both "white gospel" and "black gospel" emerged essentially through the pious efforts of highly-motivated, evangelistic singers of the early part of the Twentieth Century. Their rich legacy enthused many to sing message-music professionally.

Convention-style singing was pioneered in the American Southland by the deeply spiritual and charismatic school teacher, James D. Vaughan. His ground-breaking quartet initially was composed of him and his three brothers. After music school, taught by E. T. Hildebrand, Vaughan practised his songwriting to the full, going on to write hundreds of *easy-on-the-ear* ditties such as '*I Feel Like Travelling On*'. Theologically, Vaughan was of *Nazarene* persuasion from a *Holiness* and *Wesleyan* background. *'Gospel Chimes'* was Vaughan's first published songbook embracing the shaped note techniques. Conceived several hundred years ago and called *'Sacred Harp'*, users could recognise the *Fa, So, La* or *Mi* by reading the shape of the note on the stave.

In the USA particularly, churches of every denomination prospered in number in the first quarter of the Twentieth Century as a result of the great revivals. With their steady growth came a hunger in lay people for newer gospel songs. To meet common demand, Vaughan set up a publishing and marketing concern in Lawrenceburg, Tennessee with a network of enterprising quartets to promote the new sacred songs. By 1912, they were selling eighty-five thousand songbooks per year and by the mid Twenties there were no less than sixteen quartets on the road. Then Vaughan expanded into new even more adventurous branches of activity such as radio stations, phonograph records and singing schools. Expansion came geographically too, as the organisation extended into four other states including Texas. Basically of *Southern Baptist* persuasion, it was in Texas that the Stamps' gospel enterprise prospered mostly under the astute auspices of V.O. and Frank Stamps in the second quarter of the Twentieth Century. Later, *"their empire"* joined with the *"Baxter empire"* to form the renowned joint *"Stamps Baxter empire"*. For many years, the *"Stamps Baxter"* quartet-style of music was slow in gaining acceptance even in the South of the USA among mainstream, denominational churches.

Serious-minded evangelicals particularly in the North in the USA and in the United Kingdom were still distrustful of songs that had a beat. Some felt that the message was not deep enough, and the pentecostal theology too emotional. Groups, who failed to sing in the strict tempo that the churches expected, were distrusted. They were also distrustful of songs when themes strayed from the well-trodden orthodox path. The pentecostals were the first grouping to make widespread use of black and white *Southern gospel* music. Their emotional, enthusiasm-flavoured worship was ideally suited to using contemporary songs with a beat. In the Twenties and Thirties, this type of music was commonly heard at "All Day Sings", "Brush Arbor Meetings" and Festivals of Male Voice Praise. All were opportunities where enthusiastic Christians of several denominations would rally together. It was in such events in the Twenties that the young impressionable Blackwood Brothers were introduced to this kind of engaging music. The wholescale advent of the electronic media (including phonograph records and radio) was to explode, facilitating the expansion of gospel music. Within the time span of only one generation, gospel music eventually reached every corner of the world. The Blackwood Brothers and other groups supported the pioneer publishers and in the decades that followed pioneered the spread of Christian music across the USA. Between the two great World Wars, they put in the hands of common folk books with songs from James D. Vaughan, R. E. Winsett, *Hartford Music*, *Stamps Baxter Music*, and *Gospel Quartet Music*. These prized publications contained three major types of sacred songs, sweet solemn hymns, repetitive spirituals, and the happy, rollicking gospel songs! The spirit of these numbers inspired multitudes!

Like many established structures of society, the focus of Christian music began to dramatically change during the period after World War II and particularly in the Sixties. Society's accepted values and norms were under tremendous attack not least in morality, fashion and art-forms. It was a substantial social revolution that affected every area of culture, even ethics. Gospel music was until this time, aimed primarily at established church members. Many of the younger generation wanted something different. Suddenly, innovative sounds arose from artistes like Elvis Presley, Cliff Richard, Andrae Crouch, Second Chapter Of Acts, Jessy Dixon, Barry McGuire and many more! Contemporary composers, arrangers, and producers started writing more modern material potentially much wider in taste and scope.

The Sixties were a pivotal time in the church - the early days of the "Jesus Movement", the "Charismatic Movement", the "House Church Movement" and the "Praise and Worship Movement".

In the Seventies, performers emerged to international prominence from what became known as the *"Jesus Movement"*. On the Californian coast thousands of teens and twenties were *"turning to Christ"*. Not everyone, however, approved but the younger generation warmly embraced the changes as repertoires and arrangements illustrated. Later decades continued to push back the established cultural horizons in Christian music as a whole. Large and noteworthy gatherings started to take place such as England's Greenbelt Arts Festival and the Christian Artistes Conventions hosted in different parts of the world by the likes of pioneers like Cam Floria and Leen La Riviere of Continental Ministries. Fuelled by the new trends, by this time it was generally considered that progressively professionalism had now found its role throughout the ranks of all the growing Christian music genres. Many of the audio recording projects were now made in the hit-making studios of London, Chicago, New York, Los Angeles and in particular, Nashville. Over later decades, thousands of new recordings followed from a galaxy of many new Christian artistes with substantial God-given talent. By the Nineties it seemed that professional diversity was complete as Christian artistes foraged into the whole spectrum of styles. Meanwhile, in the UK and the USA, new festivals and conventions that majored on contemporary expressions of music prospered profusely.

History's irrepressible advances will condemn the vast majority of mankind's art and industry to be lost forever in the sands of subsequent generations. In this book in a balanced way, I have sought to subjectively and objectively select the special inspirational songs that I think, on merit are deserving of longevity. Clearly reflective of my personal taste, those songs have sufficient quality or dare I say, an eternal quality to outlive the generations that produced them. The dictionary describes a classic as a work of lasting quality. Among the ranks of inspirational music recording classics are some outstanding works and performances that justly deserve more than a dust-gathering place on the archive shelves of the great recording companies. History documents that Man's longest lasting songs are God-directed.

Relatively speaking, the audio recorded works of Mankind's music belong to recent history. Although much of what is produced may commendably serve its own generation, the majority will clearly not, and does not deserve to stand the test of time. As we commence the Third Millennium AD, these musical expressions of faith are a tangible reminder of God-honouring gospel music that can inspire those who follow. Our peers still find genuine inspiration and peaceful consolation in the music of the Twentieth Century! Singable Christian rhyme is still at the core of the British and American cultures and peoples. Despite the flagrantly permissive attitudes and actions around us, Middle-Britain and Middle-America's Christian communities are musically still generally, down-to-earth, unpretentious and happy to "wear religion on the sleeve".

Paradoxically, the Twentieth Century Christian music legacy is brimful of both the personal and impersonal, the complex and uncomplicated, the sentimental and the unsentimental. Yet it is music with a message that still tugs at the heart, moistens the eyes, and sets voices humming! It will continue to inspire generations yet unborn.

PAUL DAVIS

Abba Father, Let Me Be
Dave Bilbrough

> '*For as many as are led by the Spirit of God, they are the sons of God.*
>
> *For ye have not received the spirit of bondage again to fear; but ye have received the Spirit of adoption, whereby we cry, Abba, Father.*
>
> *The Spirit itself beareth witness with our spirit, that we are the children of God.*'
> *(Romans 8:14-16)*

A post World War II over-spill of urban population just outside London's east end, Romford, Essex is not one of the places that one would expect to find one of the most prolific of the Twentieth Century's gospel songwriters! But it's there that you will find the talented author of "Abba Father" and "Let there Be Love Shared Among Us". Coming from a humble, musical family of working class stock, fourteen years old Dave Bilbrough initially had little to do with churches of any description. Then, as he says, out of the blue he was invited to visit the local church youth group by his sister Anne (who was a Christian). *"I admit that I only attended",* Dave says, *"because of my fondness for table tennis and in the hope of meeting some nice pretty girls. But in the midst of this first experience of Christian fellowship something much deeper was stirred in my heart!"*

Worldwide, music was changing, focusing on philosophical searches of all kinds from Barry McGuire to the Beatles to Simon and Garfunkel. It caught Dave's attention. He remembers, *"I had been given a Paul Simon Songbook about the time that I visited the church youth club. I really related to his simple songs because they posed the kind of questions I wanted answers to! At the youth club epilogue I can remember someone saying that Jesus was either the greatest liar on earth, a nutcase...or else, who He said He was and there was truth in what He was saying!!"* That dramatic comment caused an already inquisitive Dave to seriously ponder for himself the issue of who Jesus was. About a year later he became a Christian.

With this new-born faith came an overwhelming desire to express himself musically. So jumping in with two feet, Dave decided to learn to play the acoustic guitar. He discovered a dusty instrument hidden in the dim cupboard under the stairs where his father had stashed it away. It needed much attention but Dave was zealous. It was duly repaired and given a fresh coat of black paint to make it look like the one Elvis Presley played! Now Dave set himself the uphill task of teaching himself the basic chords. It hurt at first, his fingers getting red and raw. Nevertheless, he persevered progressing through the elementary chords, eventually plucking up the courage to take it to the midweek Baptist Church Bible studies. His seventeen years old peers loved his guitar playing especially the girls! That encouraged him even more. Sitting on the floor, he led the self conscious group in song week by week. But he often felt that the worship-time was stilted and prayers were left to those few who could wax eloquently and poetically. There was a gaping hole between the poetic flowery words of the Victorian hymns stored in sturdy hymnals and the simple direct language used by ordinary people from Romford! Dave realised that he needed to capture a cutting edge of relevance. *"I longed for us (in the songs we were singing and the way we prayed and testified) to express ourselves more naturally and simply!"* One day, Dave's buddy, Nick Butterworth caught his attention, stimulating his vision with a challenging question. Smiling at Dave, looking him squarely in the eye, Nick spoke in all seriousness. *"Dave, you're playing that old battered guitar pretty good nowadays! Why don't you try your hand at writing some new songs for us to sing?"*

"Are you kidding Mate!!" was Dave's quick-fire, self-conscious, laughing response. But that night he tossed and turned in bed pondering whether he could try his hand at song writing. Then some real major inspiration came from a music festival where he first heard Karen Lafferty's "Seek Ye First The Kingdom of God" sung by Chuck Girard. *"Man that's great!",* Dave thought to himself, *"That's the kinda Christian music me and my mates can relate to!"*

Back home in his small bedroom, that night with his trusty guitar, Dave experimented with rhyme and melody as embryos of songs started to gestate. Times were changing in Dave's life too. He noticed that most of his teenage friends had married and suddenly, he was aware of "being left behind". *"I felt inadequate and needing the intimacy that personal faith brings! Days were tough, but I knew this was a 'pruning-time' in my life. Through it all, my desire to know the Lord more grew deeper!"*

Weeks later from this experience, the soon-to-be classic- "Abba Father"- was written in his bedroom after hearing a sermon on the subject. *"Abba",* the preacher said, *"is an Aramaic word from Bible days meaning 'father'. It's always been a customary title of God in prayer. It was found in the Babylonian Talmud where it was used, of a child to his father, and also as a type of address to rabbis! It's equivalent to 'Daddy' or 'Papa' in our culture today."*

Later Dave says he did some reading of his own on the intriguing subject. He says, *"Down the centuries, the Jews found it too presumptuous and nearly blasphemous to use the word 'Abba'. They would therefore never address God in that manner! But Christ called God 'Abba Father' and gave that same right to us, His disciples and the Apostle Paul saw 'Abba' as symbolic of our Christian adoption as children of God and of possession of the Spirit!"*

In the last quarter of the Century, the name Dave Bilbrough was truly known for trail-blazing pioneering in the blossoming contemporary British worship movement. Aided by his talented pretty wife- Pat, Dave's innovative hymns and choruses rejuvenated the jaded, banal Church music scene. The Christian public warmed to his "unfussy lyrics" and simple melodies that spoke in unpretentious terms. He says, *"'Abba Father' is a term that still can convey a sense of warmth, intimacy and respect for our Heavenly Father!...I'm still amazed when I see how 'Abba Father' is sung by Christians all over the world! The secret of its success lies, I believe, in its simplicity and honest prayer-like quality and sentiment!"*

Abba Father, let me be
Yours and Yours alone.
May my will forever be
Ever more Your own.
Never let my heart grow cold,
Never let me go.
Abba Father, let me be
Yours and Yours alone.

As We Are Gathered
John Daniels

'For where two or three are gathered together in my name,
there am I in the midst of them.'
(Matthew 18:20)

Soft-spoken English songwriter, John Daniels started his musical
ministry in the early Seventies touring the midlands of England as
part of a group called the Alethians that included pianist, David
Anfield and vocalist Dave Pope. It was a traumatic social change-
the time of the height of the Beatles success and of the Vietnam
crisis. Long entrenched attitudes were changing substantially with
the advent of contemporary Christian music. It was a movement
spearheaded by the younger generation who rightly saw themselves
as being the church of tomorrow. Young faces as well as young music
were demanded. It was also a move away from Christian performers
who overtly displayed what was seen as the unbecoming techniques
and theatrics of show-business. It was a pivotal time in the UK church
- the early days of the 'Charismatic movement', the 'House Church
movement' and the 'Praise and Worship movement'.

In every generation, the winds of change blow constantly through
all departments of life especially fashion, culture and musical taste.
In truth, the young Alethians were a combo that attacked the fashion-

culture-storms of those days with modest success. The group was short lived as Dave Pope soon emerged as one of Britain's most articulate young evangelists with a particular ministry to young people. David Anfield went on to become a very able orchestrator and record producer for artistes such as William McCrea and Wes Davis. Meanwhile, John Daniels, the more quiet of the three concentrated on what he saw as his first calling, songwriting.

John penned the gentle song-'As We Are Gathered'- to remind believers in every generation that Christ's promise is that even where merely two or three persons are gathered together in His name that He is always there in the midst of them. John Daniels says, *'That makes every Christian meeting in every generation a divine appointment! The promise of Jesus was given by Him before His death and resurrection. Then after Christ had ascended to heaven from the Mount of Olives came the miracle of Pentecost Morning in first century Jerusalem. Thousands were added to the Church of Jesus Christ daily from that day and the practice of Christian meetings from that point was established.'*

It was documented by Doctor Luke in the Acts of the Apostles that the First Century Church devoted itself to several priorities including the *'apostles' teaching'* which included all that Jesus Himself taught especially the gospel, which was centred in His death, burial and resurrection. It was a unique teaching in that it came from God and was clothed with the authority conferred on the apostles. Today it is freely available, documented in the books of the New Testament.

The First Century Church devoted itself to the corporate fellowship of believers in worship and to the *'breaking of bread'*. Although this phrase was used of an ordinary meal in homes it also spoke of the Lord's Supper. High also on the First Century Church's list of priorities was, of course, their devotion to *'prayer'*. The book of Acts emphasises the importance of prayer in the Christian life—private as well as public.

The writer, Luke describes how the First Century Church's *'believers were together'* and the unity of the early church was such that they held *'everything in common'*. This was a voluntary sharing to provide for those who did not have enough for the essentials of living.

Most interesting is the description given of how the First Century Church devoted itself to '*braking bread in their homes*'. Here in the book of Acts, the daily life of Christians is described, distinguishing their activity in the temple from that in their private homes, where they ate their meals (not the Lord's Supper) with gladness and generosity. The open hospitality of the fellowship of the First Century Church exhibited a oneness and sharing enjoyed among all believers. The fruits of the Spirit were demonstrated in great abundance, amazing the pagan Roman world. The qualities of the new Christian life lived 'in the Spirit' such as love, joy, peace and patience were now not merely preachers' slogans but were the predominant disposition of millions of believers. John Daniel's classic song-'As We Are Gathered'-spans the centuries between now and back to the First Century when the promise of Christ was first given.

As we are gathered Jesus is here;
One with each other, Jesus is here.
Joined by the Spirit, washed in the blood,
Part of the body, the church of God.
As we are gathered Jesus is here,
One with each other, Jesus is here.

At Your Feet We Fall
Dave Fellingham

> *'And when I (Apostle John) saw him (Christ), I fell at his feet as dead.*
> *And he laid his right hand upon me, saying unto me,*
> *Fear not; I am the first and the last:*
> *I am he that liveth, and was dead;*
> *and, behold, I am alive for evermore, Amen;*
> *and have the keys of hell and of death.'*
> *(Revelation 1:17-18)*

Dave Fellingham's wonderful worship chorus was inspired by the Apostle John's revelation of the Risen Jesus Christ. The Apostle received the revelation while imprisoned on Patmos, a small (four by eight miles), rocky island in the Aegean Sea some 50 miles southwest of Ephesus, off the coast of modern Turkey. It probably served as a Roman penal settlement. Eusebius, the "father of church history" (A.D. 265-340), reports that John was released from Patmos under the emperor Nerva (A.D. 96-98). To John, Christ revealed Himself as *the Alpha and the Omega,* the first and last letters of the Greek alphabet. God is the beginning and the end, sovereignly ruling over all human history.

Christ applies the title *Almighty* to Himself. Nine of the twelve occurrences of this term in the New Testament are found in Revelation. The Apostle says he was *in the Spirit on the Lord's Day.*

The *Lord's Day* is a technical term for the first day of the week—so named because Jesus rose from the dead on that day. It was also the day on which the Christians met and took up collections to help the needy. John's words, *in the Spirit* referred to a state of spiritual exaltation-not a dream, but a vision of the S*on of Man robed to His feet.* The high priest of New Testament days wore a full-length robe, thus the Apostle was referring to Christ as a high priest with a golden sash around His chest. His white like wool, hoary head suggests wisdom and dignity and His eyes like blazing fire speak of penetrating insight. His sharp double-edged sword like a long Thracian sword symbolized divine judgment.

Dave says, *"The Apostle John fell at His feet, a sign of great respect and awe! Christ then revealed Himself as the Living One, the "living God"! In gross contrast to the dead gods of paganism, Christ possesses life in His essential nature. The keys of death and Hades give Him absolute control over their domain!"*

Dave Fellingham not only writes worship music, he is also a writer of contemporary classical music, and has many works performed by orchestras, chamber groups and choirs. Eager to maintain a balanced life, Dave finds time for other things too! A very keen sports enthusiast, he enjoys playing squash, soccer and skiing. *"At home"*, he says, *"I enjoy cowboy video movies and maintain an absorbing interest in history. I also admit that I enjoy cooking-especially fish dishes! I think that garlic, peppers, mushrooms and cream, together with a little je ne sais quoi are the basis for any good meal that one can cook!"*

Dave was born in 1945 just after the end of World War II. There amid the green English environs of Horsham in Sussex, his parents served as Salvation Army officers. After several appointments with the Salvation Army, the Fellingham family finally settled down in the village of Tongham located between Aldershot and Guildford. David's young heart warmed early in life to the call of the gospel. In childlike simplicity, he remembers that he became a Christian as a young child becoming actively involved in the musical life of the local Salvation Army corps. Dressed in the traditional blue uniform of General Booth's Tongham brigade, the teenager found music and faith seemed to mix easily as he matured.

David received a useful post-war education at George Abbot School for Boys in Guildford, Surrey. Leaving after his sixth year at the School, he worked amid shelves of books as a librarian for a year. Unable to settle, he then decided to train to be a teacher. He graduated from Sussex University in 1968 with an honours degree in education. His musical giftings, however, were not forgotten.

David also became an associate with the Royal College of Music, majoring in the trumpet. In July 1968, wedding bells rang out as David married Rosemary Downer, daughter of Eric Downer who was converted under the ministry of the famous pentecostal pioneer, George Jeffreys. Eric was the secretary of the Britain's Elim Churches conference. David's employment history continued with a brief spell of teaching music at Newhaven Tideway followed by his appointment as the Director of Music at Longhill until 1976. Then he entered the Christian ministry as a lay pastor in an Anglican Church. In early 1979, he became part of the leadership team of what is now called Church of Christ the King on England's south coast. Recognised as an internationally renowned songwriter, worship leader, author and speaker, his ministry at the Church of Christ the King is primarily as an evangelist, he is also responsible for organising creative outreach events and overseeing worship within the Church. *"Together with his wife-Rosie"*, he says, *"I am involved in crisis counselling particularly in the area of spiritual deliverance."* David's Church has developed links with other churches that gives opportunity for him to minister regularly in North America, Europe and the Far East.

David and Rosemary parented two sons, Luke and Nathan. Both are now married and are part of a full-time Christian music ministry, regularly playing music at major Christian conferences worldwide.

At Your feet we fall, mighty risen Lord,
As we come before Your throne to worship You.
By Your Spirit's power You now draw our hearts,
And we hear Your voice in triumph ringing clear.

I am He that liveth, that liveth and was dead,
Behold I am alive forever more.

Be Bold, Be Strong
Morris Chapman

> *'Only be thou strong and very courageous,*
> *that thou mayest observe to do according to all the law,*
> *which Moses my servant commanded thee:*
> *turn not from it to the right hand or to the left,*
> *that thou mayest prosper whithersoever thou goest.*
> *This book of the law shall not depart out of thy mouth;*
> *but thou shalt meditate therein day and night,*
> *that thou mayest observe to do according to all that is written*
> *therein: for then thou shalt make thy way prosperous,*
> *and then thou shalt have good success.*
> *Have not I commanded thee?*
> *Be strong and of a good courage; be not afraid, neither be*
> *thou dismayed: for the LORD thy God is with thee*
> *whithersoever thou goest.*
> *(Joshua 1:7-8)*

Morris Chapman was a rural Arkansas boy who grew up to eschew the city glamour of Las Vegas and followed the Lord's leading into a gospel music ministry. He told me, *"I have just one desire, I want only one thing out of life; to be a blessing to others that they may know my Lord as Saviour as I do!"* Taking on his Divine vocation called for Morris to step out boldly into what God had planned for him. This motivated his greatest song, inspired by the Jewish hero-Joshua (whose given name meant "salvation").

Initially born in Egyptian bondage (c. 1500 BC), years later-two months after Israel's exodus-he was appointed Moses' army commander and successfully resisted an Amalekite attack. Joshua changed his name to mean "Jehovah is salvation", the meaning in Greek is Jesus. Later as the representative of the tribe of Ephraim in spying out Canaan, Joshua opposed the spies' pessimistic majority report. He insisted that if Israel was faithful to God, she could conquer Canaan! He almost suffered stoning for his trust in God. For having "followed the Lord wholeheartedly", he not only escaped destruction but also received assurance from God, unique to himself and Caleb, of entering the Promised Land.

About 40 years later, God designated Joshua as Moses' successor. After Moses' death, came the appearance of "the commander of the army of the Lord"-the visible confirmation of Joshua's divine call. He then faithfully executed the God-directed siege. The Lord initiated the action by charging Joshua to *"be bold, be strong for the Lord your God is with you!"* God promised success-but only if Israel obeyed God. Accordingly, the city of Jericho was destroyed and within six years Joshua took the whole land.

Morris Chapman was born in Camden, Arkansas in 1938, one of twelve children. His musical influences came mainly from listening regularly to artists like Joy May and Rosetta Tharpe on the radio. His earliest musical ambition was to learn to play the piano but money in the Chapman household was short and did not stretch to providing Morris with his desire. His father worked in the local paper mill. This added to the meagre income he earned from farming.

Amid economic stress, the family's social life revolved around the local church. It was there that Morris was encouraged to use his initiative and to be bold and strong.

Boldly, he asked if he could teach himself to play the piano located in the church building. *"Permission granted"*, he laughingly remembered, *"I would go every day after school and just make noises. I experimented with the various notes until eventually I taught myself to make what could be termed 'music'!* As my proficiency grew, I was permitted to play the piano and organ for the church services, all the time growing ever more proficient."

Dropping out of school in the tenth grade, he found work as a janitor and dishwasher. These and other odd jobs helped with the family finances. Maurice recalls how in those days a prophecy was said over his older sister that promised that in time the whole family would move to a distant city! *"My older sister moved first to Las Vegas and sent me the money to join her in 1957, starting our whole family exodus!"* He continued, *"Thankfully ,the Lord gave us a new home. As each of us became established, we sent the next family member the money to make the move! At one time, we all worked for the Las Vegas school system. The family provided three teachers, one head of purchasing and one dean of students!"* When Morris first arrived in glitzy Las Vegas, it was at a time when it was becoming the gambling capital of the world. He found a job as a porter at the famous Flamingo Hotel, but it was not the bright lights of the show business world that attracted him. Rather it was the music ministry of his local church! Soon he became choir director and organist-pianist of the Upper Room Church of God in Christ. Morris says, *"I credit Andrae Crouch with being my early gospel music inspiration after Andrae and his first group-The Cogics- did a concert in the church that truly thrilled and motivated me in the music ministry!"*

Initially, the lure of earning big money playing the piano in one of the numerous casinos proved a temptation for Morris. *"But after a few days"*, he says, *"I realised how empty it all was! I played for famed black gospel artiste Clara Ward for a time at the Hacienda and for other gospel groups passing through town. But I did not feel right about it!"*

Morris married when he was twenty one years of age. A job opportunity arose in the local school that helped to provide for his family. He says, *"I faithfully stayed there for seventeen years before God finally told me that it was time for me to start a full time gospel music ministry."*

During those seventeen years, Morris began to experiment in composing gospel songs. Eventually in 1976, he started receiving invitations to sing in churches far away from his Las Vegas home. *"I would work week days in the school then travel every weekend to appear in venues away from home. It was in 1978 when I appeared at a Full Gospel Businessmen's Prayer Breakfast in Houston, Texas that I decided the time for change had come! Returning home, I announced to my wife and family that I felt the Lord was calling me into full time ministry!"*

The next exciting step in Morris' career came in the form of the singing songwriter and record producer- Gary S. Paxton. Gary became very excited about the Chapman songs and set about producing a demo record for Morris entitled "The Lord Reigns!" At the same time, Morris received a ticket from an unknown benefactor for a twenty one day tour to the Holy Land with a group. While he was away, Gary Paxton got down to work on his behalf and submitted the demo to Word's Myrrh Records. The company agreed to sign the new performer on his return from Israel and release the demo as an album in 1980. The Holy Land tour proved to be an inspirational experience for Morris and one of his most well known songs ("Bethlehem Morning"), was inspired by a visit to that little town.

"On my return", Morris remembers, *"my Christian music career blossomed with tours all over the USA, Australia, Europe and third world countries. My unique brand of traditional and contemporary style of music was vocally compared to soul singer Lou Rawls. But I tried to make my music acceptable to people in both the black and white gospel music scenes!"*

Be bold, be strong!
For the Lord your God is with you.
Be bold, be strong!
For the Lord your God is with you.
I am not afraid,
I am not dismayed,
Because I'm walking in faith and victory,
Come on and walk in faith and victory,
For the Lord your God is with you.

Because He Lives
Bill & Gloria Gaither

'I am come that they might have life, and that they might have it more abundantly!' (John 10:10)
'Because I live, ye shall live also.' (John 14:19)

Married in the early Sixties, at the height of the paranoia of fear caused by the Cold War stand-off between the Allies and the Soviets, Bill and Gloria Gaither were soon facing the birth of their first child. At breakfast time, peering over the morning newspaper with a look of anguish, the heavily pregnant Gloria read aloud the headlines to her spouse. She spoke of Moscow's latest frightening announcement of yet a further escalation of atomic weaponry between the super powers. *"How can we face bringing a child into a world like this, Bill?"*

"Because He lives, Honey! Life is still worth the living!" Bill's response was measured and calm. He was in the process of recovering from a debilitating bout of mononucleosis. *"It's at times like these, Gloria, that we can testify that our new life in Jesus provides trusting believers with a wonderfully fulfilling life, now and for Eternity!"*

"You're right, Bill! The scripture promises that our times are in His hands!...Yes, because He lives, we can face tomorrow!...I feel a song comin' on! What an exciting theme for an Easter song!" Indeed very soon, the first two verses of *"Because He lives"* took shape.

The song lay unfinished until Gloria's father died and the song was completed with the emotional but triumphal third verse about seeing the lights of glory.

Songwriters, Bill and Gloria since then are heralded by many among the greatest hymn writers of history because of songs like *"Because He lives"* and *"He Touched Me"*. The duo wrote this song when part of a trio that included Bill's brother, Danny.

Born 28 March 1936, Bill grew up in Alexandria, a rural area of Indiana. Coming from such a down-to-earth, farming family, he told me that he learned to take pleasure in the everyday essential farm jobs like milking the cows. *"I think this helped"*, he declared, *"as far as what I'm doing today in songwriting. It's helped me develop a sensitivity to life and for the caring of the new-born. When someone speaks about simple, everyday things I know what they're talking about!"* Bill never planned to take up farming as a career because as he jokingly says, *"I have always had a bad case of hay fever! That's always been a problem to me even as a child working outside!"*

A country boy, Bill always loved sacred music. But he gave up the idea of making it a serious career after high school. He thought he was not good enough to do it full-time. Bill was fourteen years old when he first heard the Blackwood Brothers' Quartet on record, as he explained to me, he became captivated! *"As a boy I cannot begin to tell you the impression those records made on my young life. I could not wait to get home from school in the evening to play them. I had many dreams to one day be able to sing like that! In those days, there were not that many opportunities for a young person interested in full-time music. So I went to college and majored in English. Later, I taught English in public high school for seven or eight years, planning to do that for the rest of my life. That's where I met my wife Gloria. She was also teaching school at the same place. The thing that stopped my teaching career was when we started writing original songs together."*

Nowadays, people sometimes ask, *"Where does the poetry come from in your music?"* Bill replies, *"Well, I think it has to be born in you! I think you can fan the spark, but there must be a natural inclination to understand poetic things, understand the power of poetic suggestion, and to understand signals. I've often said I think everybody has to have a little bit of poetry in him to even make it these days!'* Surprisingly, Bill says that he never found himself coming top of the class in things like poetry and his school friends would now be amazed at the way he has developed this talent. Gloria Sickal (his wife-to-be) was born in Battle Creek, Michigan on 4 March 1942. She was far more academic than Bill and graduated from Anderson College with honours in French, English and Sociology.

In the last quarter of the Twentieth Century, the Gaithers wrote several hundred successful gospel songs. That's not a lot when compared to Charles Wesley and Fanny Crosby who wrote thousands! Time, however, is on the Gaithers' side, grace permitting! The great songwriters of previous generations, of course, came to their greatest attention after they were gone. With the power of today's media available, the Gaithers have become a legend in their lifetimes. Their repertoire has been recorded by almost every quality artist who has ever warbled a gospel song from Elvis Presley to Pat Boone to George Hamilton IV to Johnny Cash to George Beverly Shea.

I asked Bill how it made him feel to be classed among the ranks of history's great hymn writers. *"You know",* Bill modestly stated, *"in something as sensitive as Christian ministry I don't think one can even think about that very long because the Lord blesses and the Lord adds to the increase. The only reason we are here in the first place is because God chose to bless the ministry!'* I then asked whether the pressure of success dulls the edge of their spiritually. Bill spoke positively on this matter. *"There are basic tenets of our faith that are big! They are the theological principles that we believe and hear from the pulpit every Sunday. ..The basic objective of our ministry is how to put heavy theological ideas that we all believe, into everyday terms that make a difference in people's day to day lives and decisions!'* To their credit the Gaithers have been uncompromising in their approach to their music ministry down through the years. They have maintained a consistency and an integrity that have helped them to remain spiritually sharp and culturally relevant.

God sent His Son, they called Him Jesus!
He came to love, heal and forgive,
He lived and died to buy my pardon,
An empty grave is there to prove my Saviour lives!
Because He lives, I can face tomorrow;
Because He lives all fear is gone;
Because I know He holds the future,
And life is worth the living just because He lives!

Bless The Lord, O My Soul
Andrae Crouch

'Bless the LORD, O my soul: and all that is within me, bless his holy name.
Bless the LORD, O my soul, and forget not all his benefits:
Who forgiveth all thine iniquities; who healeth all thy diseases;
Who redeemeth thy life from destruction; Who crowneth thee with lovingkindness and tender mercies; Who satisfieth thy mouth with good things; so that thy youth is renewed like the eagle's.'
(Psalm 103:1-5)

Andrae Crouch told me that he first received the divine call into the gospel music ministry at the tender age of eleven! About that time, his father Rev. Benjamin Crouch was managing the east Los Angeles family cleaning business whilst also preaching on the streets of the city at weekends. Subsequently, Benjamin was called to take on the full time pastorship of a small church. Initially, he was somewhat reluctant to take the position partly because the church did not have an available pianist. Andrae remembers, *"Dad called me up in front of the surprised congregation and asked me publicly that if God would give me the gift of music, would I use it for the rest of my life to His glory? When I said 'Yes!', he prayed for me and I knew right then that God was going to do something special in my life!"*

Within a week a tremendous miracle had taken place, young Andraé was playing age-old hymns on his newly acquired piano from a local lady who felt led to donate to the local church. Instantly, Andrae became the church's new pianist under his father's new pastorship. The fledgling church was zealous but poor. Therefore, the small congregation had no hymnals to sing from. Seizing the opportunity, the resourceful Andrae used his God-given, personal ability to "play by ear" and pitched his new, easy-to-sing songs to the surprised congregation and soloists. Very soon the song material penned by Andrae increased in popularity. His undoubted skills began to be noticed further afield.

Andrae had become a born again Christian one Sunday night under the preaching of his enthusiastic father. *"I remember"*, Andrae says, *"I sat there in the church congregation listening under conviction. When father finally gave the invitation I willingly went forward. I just felt so close to the Lord...I cried and cried...Then when everybody started singing, I was so happy!...I started jumping around the church and split my new shoes!"*

With great expectation, Andrae left college in 1965. He soon formed his own vocal group-The Disciples. Together, they enjoyed considerable local success and helped popularise Andrae's repertoire. At about this time, the Los Angeles Teen Challenge Center offered him a position in their growing organisation. The work among drugs addicts was tough and demanding. But he hesitated as Andrae knew that his commitment to the Christian vision was not absolute. He says, *"It took several months of soul searching before I finally ceased my struggle and committed my life wholly to the Lord and His service. Joining Teen Challenge, I formed a choir (from among the drug addicts) that performed regularly in the Southern Californian area. While at Teen Challenge, the Lord really put a burden on my heart for needy people everywhere. I saw the good effect my music had on people that didn't know the Lord personally. So I began to write more songs that would be a blessing to others."*

National then international doors started to open and soon Andrae's unique song-writing ability became appreciated from shore to shore in many areas of the globe's vast gospel music spectrum. Christian people fell in love with Andrae and his songs like "Bless

The Lord". The repertoire was as much at home in "Southern Gospel" conventions as it was in his "Black Gospel" music circles. Folk everywhere in progressive and traditional churches seemed to recognise Andrae's God-given ability to marry a heart-warming melody with powerful subtle, theological lyrics.

Thus his songbook produced many of the Century's most familiar black gospel hit songs. One of his earliest and most popular was "Bless The Lord", a paraphrase of Psalm 103. The original words of this Jewish Psalm formed a hymn that told of God's love and compassion toward His ancient people. It was the same "call to praise" that also framed the body of Andrae's hymn and set its tone. The often repeated phrase "O my soul" was a conventional Hebrew way of addressing oneself . It made the receiving of blessings personal, calling upon believers to "bless the Lord!" for all the personal benefits received from the Divine Hand. Then followed a recollection of God's mercies towards His people. The song celebrates God's ongoing mercy and compassion on His people, proclaiming the vastness of His love and its unending perseverance.

Bless the Lord, O my Soul,
Bless the Lord, O my soul,
And all that is within me
Bless His holy name.

Blessed Assurance
Fanny Crosby

'That their hearts might be comforted, being knit together in love, and unto all riches of the full assurance of understanding, to the acknowledgement of the mystery of God, and of the Father, and of Christ;
In whom are hid all the treasures of wisdom and knowledge.'
(Colossians 2:2-3)

Fanny Crosby's life ended in 1915, a year after the start of World War I. Fully persuaded of deep scriptural truths, her long life radiated, the "blessed assurance" she enjoyed. More than any other contemporary songwriter, she captured the heart of the Gospel in her simple, meaningful songs. In turn, she captured the hearts of millions! She devoted her long, fruitful life to two main pursuits. Firstly, she served the dropouts and drunks of New York's inner city missions. Secondly, she devoted herself to the ministry of transposing the great spiritual truths into singable rhyme and melody.

Despite the tragedy of blindness, never self-pitying, her rich hymnal expressions were lived out in a remarkably normal life. She demonstrated a matter of fact confidence in Christ. The "poor little blind girl" became a highly competent poet of world-wide influence with a stunning memory, her poems were composed and edited in her mind then dictated. She rose to be a social guest of six USA presidents yet she humbly accepted only about two dollars for each of her compositions, deliberately choosing to live simply and soberly. Her songs outsold secular hits of the day such as *"In The Good Old Summertime"*, *"When You And I Were Young Maggie"* and *"Silver Threads Among The Gold"*. If there had been a pop chart in those days, she would be a regular at the top.

Her many distinguished associates included such people as Dwight L Moody-the evangelist and his song leader-Ira Sankey. Her emotion-tugging songs translated into many languages attracted world attention. Countless celebrated recording artistes throughout the last Century articulated her song material , some of whom devoted concept albums to solely her compositions including Pat Boone, Eddy Arnold and George Hamilton IV.

Mrs. Francis Jane Crosby Van Alstyne was born on 24 March 1820 and died on 12 February 1915, just forty days before her 95th birthday. Her legacy was approximately 9,000 hymns and poems, over sixty of which are still in common church usage throughout the globe in the new millennium. She had every reason it seems to be bitter with her fortune. Born of humble stock in Putnam County, New York State, baby Frances gazed around her, absorbing the colour and texture that surrounded her. Then tragedy struck...

Sadly, at six weeks old she developed an eye infection and the local unqualified doctor was urgently called. In error, he foolishly prescribed a hot mustard poultice to be placed on her inflamed eyes. This incorrect treatment blinded her for life. Despite the handicap, she was converted to Christ at an early age. Hungering and thirsting after spiritual truth, she wholeheartedly surrendered herself (including her so-called handicap of blindness) to her Saviour. In return, she was given two wonderful gifts. The first was spiritual sight, with clear spiritual vision she gazed on truths that Christless eyes never see. Secondly, she was gifted with the ability to simply express the truths she perceived in rhyme and melody. Her life-long aspiration would be to serve the Saviour she saw clearly by faith.

Gathering every cent they could muster, her dear family plagued by guilt and remorse for what the medical blunder had done to her sight, sent her to New York to see the noted eye surgeon, Dr. Valentine Mott. Perhaps, he could offer a cure for her blindness. After careful examination of her eyes, the surgeon turned to her parents and said,

"I'm sorry there's nothing I can do for this poor little blind girl!" Tragedy was turned to triumph as her visual disability drew her more closely to the Saviour she loved. Casting aside any thought of her blindness as a handicap, Fanny simply got on with her life! Using her talents for the Lord in the way she knew best , her first song appeared in print when she was only eight years old! Even in youth, Fanny evidently enjoyed a closeness to her Saviour. This divine fellowship became the anchor of her life and her songwriting inspiration.

She entered the New York School For The Blind at the age of twelve, becoming a very successful scholar. One of her teachers, Grover Cleveland later become a USA President. At the age of 27, she was invited back to become a teacher. It was there that she met the man who in 1858 was to become her husband, blind teacher and fellow musician, Alexander Van Alstyne. Resident in New York for most of her lifetime, she was personally involved in the city's downtown missions. She toiled faithfully and diligently among the ghettos' poor, needy and deprived. Being handicapped so early in life, she could keenly identify, empathise and sympathise with the under-privileged and disadvantaged of society. A champion of second-class citizens, she knew a personal life-changing encounter with the Lord Jesus Christ could bring new life and purpose.

In spite of being physically blind almost all her songs refer to seeing, watching and looking. She took Christ's command "to watch and pray" seriously becoming a keen advocate of holy, disciplined living. She declared, *"My eyes of faith are always acutely vigilant. As a Christian, I remain alert, enthusiastic in the work of the Master in view of His soon return. Among the many blessings that the Returning Christ will bring will be peace and joy to a dying world. His Coming will give hearing to the deaf, healing to the lame and not least, sight for the blind!"*

Blessèd Assurance, Jesus is mine:
O what a foretaste of glory divine!
Heir of salvation, purchase of God;
Born of His Spirit, washed in His blood.

This is my story, this is my song,
Praising my Saviour all the day long.
This is my story, this is my song,
Praising my Saviour all the day long.

Perfect submission, perfect delight,
Visions of rapture burst on my sight;
Angels descending bring from above
Echoes of mercy, whispers of love.

Perfect submission, all is at rest,
I in my Saviour am happy and blessed;
Watching and waiting, looking above,
Filled with His goodness, lost in His love.

Fanny J. Crosby arr. by Wes Davis/New Music Enterprises)
Copyright © pauldavis@newmusic28.freeserve.co.uk Used by permission

Born Again
Andrew Culverwell

> *'Jesus answered, Verily, verily, I say unto thee,*
> *Except a man be born of water and of the Spirit,*
> *he cannot enter into the kingdom of God.*
> *That which is born of the flesh is flesh;*
> *and that which is born of the Spirit is spirit.*
> *Marvel not that I said unto thee, Ye must be born again.'*
> *(John 3:5-7)*

The daily painful process of natural birth is a commonplace yet miraculous event. It is the wonder of the bringing forth of a separate new life into the natural world, accompanied by rending pain because of Eve's sin. Almost all the Biblical uses of the word "travail" point to the intense maternal suffering of birth. But Christ spoke of "a second birth" or a "new birth" being necessary to inherit eternal life. It was a theme that inspired England's Andrew Culverwell to write a hit song, the success of which surprised him as it traversed oceans! Andrew says, *"Throughout history, natural birthdays were rightly celebrated in most families and ceremonies of celebration observed at childbirth. But a Christian's second birth or new birth should also be celebrated! That's what my song 'Born Again' is all about! After all, to inherit eternal life is something worth celebrating!"* Through the last Century, *"Born Again"* was an evangelistic favourite, recorded by many people from home and abroad.

American-Norwegian songstress, Evie Tornquist Karlsson often sang it in Billy Graham Missions while the Swedish male quartet-The Samuelsons-even sang the song on their gospel trips behind the Iron Curtain. It became a great enduring Southern Gospel favourite too. The TV host-Bill Gaither in 1999 invited Evie to sing *'Born Again'* on one of his most popular videos which was broadcast worldwide.

Andrew Culverwell was born in sunny Somerset in the green picturesque West Country of England. He was the youngest of seven children and, as he put it to me, *"the only one with a Bible name and the only one in the ministry!"* It was in this environment that he committed his life to the Lord. "*The Lord really called me very young. I gave my heart to Him at the age of five and He kept me during my school days!"* What Andrew little knew then was that the world was a tough battlefield and that it was necessary for him to stand firm and grow in his new-found faith. Despite the young age and the troubles to come, the experience of spiritual "new birth" was something that he never forgot, the stimulus of his hit song written many years later.

Leaving school in great optimism at sixteen years of age, Andrew went to London to make his fortune by initially studying acting in a stage school. *"During that time"*, he says, *"I got involved with things that are better not talked about! I returned home disillusioned and confused. Home in Somerset , back to my local church, I was back in a position where God could speak to me! There in that little church, I had an emotional experience of sensing the Lord's presence in a new, very tangible way. So at the age of seventeen, I re-committed my life to the Lord!"*

With this sincere re-commitment, God opened to Andrew an exciting vision of how positively he could be used as a musical servant for the Kingdom of Heaven. Singing and playing the piano in worship services in his home church, soon Andrew's considerable musical talents came to the fore. His personal interest in Christian music was unqualified, surpassing any interest in sport or pop music. He later formed an evangelistic music group called the Four Kingsmen. They travelled widely with the radio evangelist, Eric Hutchings and his musicians, Russell and Betty Lou Mills. During all this time to provide for rent and board, Andrew also worked in the Clark Shoes Factory in Somerset, pursuing music only during his spare time.

In 1968 Andrew's church pastor invited him to visit the USA. It was the impetus he needed, he left his day job going full time into Christian music ministry. Andrew says, *"The American people welcomed me with open arms! I was delighted to see my ministry grow. So I decided to settle in the USA."*

He and his spouse, Sue (and daughters Annabelle and Sarah) located to Atlanta, Georgia. There he steadily developed his songwriting, writing hit songs like *'Born Again'* and the great Christmas favourite, *'Come On Ring Those Bells'* (recorded by Doug Oldham, Walt Mills, the Gaither Homecoming Friends and others).

He stated, *"At home, we have a music room and tape machines where my wife, Sue and I enquire of the Lord for our songs...We boldly ask Him who the song is for! I am not talking about artistes but whether for instance, the song is for 'the individual on the street' or 'the person in the church' or for 'a troubled saint'! We get before the Lord and say, 'Lord, what do you want to say through us in this song?"*

Andrew takes his songwriting ministry very seriously. *"To me"*, he says, *"it is a vocational call on my life! I feel I have a definite ministry to the church! That is those who are believers and require encouragement!...Mine is an edification ministry primarily to Christian people and my concerts whilst having an evangelistic outreach are mainly for the encouragement and the edification of the church! 'Born Again' is a testimony sermon told-in-song about a person's realising that he is a sinner needing, as Christ Jesus said, to be born again by the Spirit of God!...My heart's motivation is 'mercy' in my ministry because I know how wonderfully merciful the Lord has been to me! We're not here on earth to be better than someone else! All of us who have received the Lord's mercy should be seeking to glorify Him! Some people might think that's super-spiritual but it's not! It's humbling to realise that in these last days Almighty God can somehow communicate with human beings though a person like me! He cares about all human beings and wants us all to be re-born as His children!...I think that's incredible!"*

Born Again! There's really been a change in me,
Born Again! Just like Jesus said.
Born Again! And all because of Calvary,
I'm glad, so glad that I've been born again.

One man came to Jesus, John and Chapter three,
So afraid, O so afraid.
'Master you're from God, I really do believe'
And Jesus said, 'Be born again!'

El Shaddai
John Thompson & Michael Card

*'After these things the word of the LORD came unto Abram in
a vision, saying, Fear not, Abram: I am thy shield, and thy
exceeding great reward.*
(Genesis 15:1)

This deeply inspired and inspiring song brings vivid Old Testament
imagery alive in New Testament hymnology. "El-Shaddai" (written
by John Thompson and Michael Card) is a tribute to the all powerful
attributes of the Creator and Sustainer of the wide universe and His
great plan of salvation. Co-writer-Michael Card was born and raised
in Nashville, Tennessee. He says that the influences of Music City
USA and a close family moulded the character of his youth. His
grandfather was a Carolina preacher, his mother played classical
violin and his father, the jazz trombone. The youngest of three
children, his brother and sister also played musical instruments.

Professional musicians and performers around him in Music City
gave him firsthand expert knowledge. His boyhood buddies included
Steve and Randy Scruggs. Their father, Earl (of Flatt and Scruggs
fame) was known as the King of the Banjo Men. Lester Flatt and
Earl Scruggs provided the musical accompaniment to the Sixties
successful TV comedy series entitled "The Beverly Hillbillies" and
the cult gangster movie, "Bonnie And Clyde". As a child Michael
remembered the special attention given him as Mr Scruggs took him
aside and taught him to play banjo.

At high school, Michael also buddied up with Dale Maphis. His parents, Rose and Joe Maphis were also Country Music legends. Joe Maphis was known as King of The Strings for his outstanding guitar-playing both solo and in duet with Merle Travis. Michael recalls being around the Maphis household, loving their music. He detected that the same creative spark in them was in him too. He recalls exciting front porch jam sessions with Randy Scruggs and the Nitty Gritty Dirt Band plus enthralling visits backstage to the famed Grand Ole Opry radio show. While still in his youth, Michael became proficient on piano, guitar, banjo, violin and dulcimer. He matured early into a seasoned musician and after playing bluegrass as a kid, he progressed to rock 'n' roll as a teenager in a high school band entitled "Bubba and the Stingrays".

Enrolling at Western Kentucky University, he pursued a course in Biblical Studies thinking that God wanted him to be a teacher. *"Philosophically"*, he says, *"I did end up teaching via my music and songwriting! Back then, I developed a desire to get people interested in reading the Bible for themselves!"* His vocational direction and training came from Dr. William Lane, a professor who profoundly affected Michael's future life and career. Studying Old Testament Rabbinics under Dr. Lane, Michael hitched his studies to his music. Dr. Lane also preached at a small Presbyterian church in Bowling Green, Kentucky. Aware of his young protege's talent the professor invited Michael to write special music for the weekly services. Each week the sermon topic and text were given to Michael and from them he would write a new suitable song. The grateful congregation merely numbered about twenty people but the young troubadour was faithful to his modest task. His love of scripture became the basis of his song writing.

He modestly says, *"After a powerful experience as a thinking adult in full control of my faculties, I felt it was natural that I should use my developing music skills to communicate the reality of his growing faith. My music is like the warm touch of the morning sun. It gently awakens individual faith from its dormancy causing it to bloom anew!"*

After graduation, in the Spring of 1981 with BS and MA degrees in biblical studies, he intended to pursue his doctorate in Old

Testament Rabbinics at Cambridge University in England. Providentially, however, Randy Scruggs made contact informing Michael about the formation of a new record production company. *"Hey, Michael, how'd you feel about me and John Thompson going into the studio and you allowing us to produce some songs for you? It'll give me something to play to the record companies of my production skills and it'll also showcase your great songs, buddy!"* Excited with the prospect, the two duly met and selected two of Michael's original compositions to record. Taking them to the record companies, they were primarily meant to be a demonstration of John and Randy's skills as record producers and not Michael's skills as a performer and songwriter! Response was positive, however, about both! Soon a record company who liked the production work and the unique songs requested a whole Scruggs' album production of Card songs. So with producer, John Thompson (the co-writer of "El Shaddai") came some classic songs such as "El Shaddai" and "I Have Decided To Live Like A Believer" later to be covered by Amy Grant and Bill Gaither. Now suddenly, Michael was contending strongly for the coveted Gospel Music Association Dove Awards.

In the new millennium, Michael's repertoire covers a spectrum of styles ranging from soft ballads to high energy rock to hymns and even to folky bluegrass. A great enthusiast, he has tours internationally as a concert soloist and with a band. *"When you play your songs for an audience'*, he states, *'it's like laying part of your heart out for people. My songs are personal interpretations of the Bible. What I try to do is to interact with whatever text a song is based. I interact with my imagination and try to fill-out the theme. You have to make the message your own somehow! I find that there is always a timelessness in the thoughtful musical packaging of the Message."*

In the last two decades of the Twentieth Century, Michael matured into a contemporary folk-gospel troubador for "deeply thinking people"! His light-folky presentations promote clean cut, wholesome Christian values and reveal a depth of hymnal-theology rare to the contemporary scene. "El Shaddai" gained the status of reaching church hymnals, a creditable achievement remembering his young age. *El Shaddai"*, he says, *"is the name of God (translated 'God*

Almighty') by which He appeared to Abraham, Isaac, and Jacob). Often "the Almighty" (Shaddai without El) is also used in scripture as a name of God!" Michael concludes that the comprehension of God's truth is always a great reason to rejoice!

> *EL-SHADDAI, El-Shaddai,*
> *El-Elyon na Adonai,*
> *Age to age You're still the same*
> *By the power of the Name.*
> *El-Shaddai, El-Shaddai,*
> *Erkamka na Adonai,*
> *We will praise and lift You high.*
> *El-Shaddai.*

> *Through Your love and through the ram*
> *You saved the son of Abraham;*
> *Through the power of Your hand,*
> *Turned the sea into dry land.*
> *To the outcast on her knees*
> *You were the God who really sees,*
> *And by Your might You set Your children free.*

Father God I Wonder (I Will Sing Your Praises)
Ian Smale

'And because ye are sons, God hath sent forth the Spirit of his
Son into your hearts, crying, Abba, Father.
   Wherefore thou art no more a servant, but a son; and if a
son, then an heir of God through Christ.'
(Galatians 4:6-7)

According to scripture, God is "Father" in more ways than one! In a
special and unique sense, He is the Father of Jesus Christ. But
generally, he is known as the Father-Creator of the universe and of
the human race. The New Testament also declares that He is also the
Father who begets and takes care of His born-again believers making
them His spiritual children. It is that special relationship of father
and son that Ian Smale's beautiful chorus addresses.

The sometimes outrageous, outspoken composer of this
composition- Ian Stuart Smale (also known as Ishmael, after an Old
Testament character)-was born *10 August 1949*. Raised in Sussex,
England, his parents were Christians but the growing Ishmael was
uninterested in the church. An enthusiastic, tough rugby player, he
preferred to use his singing talents in his local pub singing bawdy
rugby songs after the matches than to point his songs heavenward!
His devoted parents, however, kept on earnestly praying for their
wayward son and their prayers were rewarded.

"One Christmas", Ishmael remembers with great conviction,
"God revealed Himself personally to me! That made all the

difference!...Then in the Seventies I started singing for the Lord and I believe I was one of the first full-time contemporary gospel artists in England!" Now highly motivated, Ishmael was soon joined in his radical music ministry by his friend, Andy Piercy and together they formed the duo known as Ishmael and Andy. They sang together successfully for three years and saw many young people brought to active faith during their revolutionary ministry. The duo then decided to go their separate ways. Ishmael went to study Christianity and its implementation at Bible College. Andy stayed in contemporary music co-founding the successful "After the Fire" band. Greats heights of critical acclaim with Epic Records were achieved by the band after much heralded accomplishments at the Greenbelt Arts Festivals of the Seventies and Eighties.

Leaving Bible college, Ishmael pastored a small Elim Pentecostal Church for two years before resuming his full time musical career. *"I felt God definitely telling me to go back on the road again and form my own band!"* The bold band, Ishmael United, consisted of Pete Wills (drums), Laurie Mellor (bass guitar), and Dave Evans (keyboards and lead guitar). At the time of their inception their impactive sound was described as "new wave" but Andy wanted to concentrate on an even more rock-sound style. Sound was not the main priority. As Ian said, *"Some musicians seem most interested in what they sound like. But to me the most important thing was getting the message of Jesus across!"*

Ishmael United recorded several innovative, almost outrageous, Christian albums including "Ready Salted", "Charge Of The Light Brigade" and "It's Amazing What Praisin' Can Do!" As well as teens and twenties, Ishmael's style of music became a big hit with junior school age youngsters. His radical approach raised criticisms and controversies during those years. Ironically, Ishmael is likely to be remembered most for bequeathing to the Century a timeless, prayerful praise-chorus. His tender composition-"Father God I Wonder"-majored on the theological subject of the Fatherhood of God and His care for His children.

Ishmael's biblical namesake bore the Hebrew name that means *"God hears"*. He was the illegitimate son of Abraham by Hagar, the Egyptian maid of his wife Sarah. Sarah was barren and in accordance with the custom of the age, gave to Abraham her handmaid Hagar as his concubine, hoping that he might obtain a family by her. When Hagar saw that she had conceived, she began to despise her mistress. Sarah made things so difficult for Hagar that she fled. Somewhere on the road to Egypt, the angel of the Lord met her and told her to return to her mistress and submit herself to her. God encouraged her with a promise of many descendants subsequently fulfilled by the Arab nations. After the weaning of Isaac, Sarah urged Abraham to get rid of Ishmael and his slave mother. Sent away with merely bread and a bottle of water, Ishmael and his mother wandered about in the wilderness of Beersheba. The angel of the Lord appeared to her, directing her to some water and renewing his former promise of Ishmael's future greatness. Ishmael was duly circumcised when he was thirteen years of age and scripture records that Father Abraham loved his son.

Father God, I wonder how I managed to exist
Without the knowledge of Your parenthood and Your loving care.
But now I am Your son, I am adopted in Your family,
And I can never be alone,
'Cause Father God, You're there beside me.
I will sing Your praises,
I will sing Your praises,
I will sing Your praises,
Forever more.

Fill The Place Lord With Your Glory
Chris Bowater

> *'And I will shake all nations, and the desire of all nations shall come: and I will fill this house with glory, saith the LORD of hosts.*
> *(Haggai 2:7)*

The beloved British singer-songwriter, Chris Bowater never realised when he commenced his worship-leading ministry in the early Seventies that over the decades to follow, he would be producing quality recording albums, books, and worship songs. To his great surprise, many of his God-directed compositions have achieved inclusion in church hymnals in various parts of the world. Before the close of the last Century, popular worship songs such as "Reign In Me", "Here I am", "Holy Spirit, We Welcome You" and "Jesus Shall Take The Highest Honour" established him as a songwriter of classic status.

Born on 2 May 1947 in Birmingham, Chris' parents were involved in Church planting and pastored whilst remaining in secular employment. Conversion came to Chris at a Youth for Christ meeting in Birmingham Town Hall in 1955. Graduating from the Royal College of Music in London in 1968, he developed a specific interest in song composition and music conducting. Chris says, *"During my student years, I seriously compromised my faith and commitment.*

Praise God that it was graciously restored before the end of my education years." With a post graduate qualification in Education from Birmingham University in 1969, he became a school teacher and taught in Birmingham, Solihull and Lincoln. This valuable teaching experience honed his communication skills and strengthened his ability to integrate contemporary music with more traditional styles. Apart from his home church commitments, he saw himself as a facilitator in his international seminar and conference work. Desiring to remain sincere and relevant, Chris aimed his sanctified art at a wide age group appeal.

Hitting the road, he travelled extensively as a performing artist, worship leader and conference speaker. But he never strayed permanently from his home base in the enterprising New Life Christian Fellowship of Lincoln, England. At this large local church, he was an enthusiastic member of Pastor Stuart Bells' leadership team. In this local church context, Chris gained considerable experience over many years in the leadership of house groups and area congregations. He delighted also in his role as the "Director of the School of Creative Ministries" that took him throughout the five continents. Chris' distinctive song-compositions are translated into scores of foreign languages, a fact that gives him great pleasure and fulfilment.

Constantly seeking to explore the vanguard of contemporary music, he was also zealous to honour the best of the hymnal heritage tradition. Consequently, his recording albums and compositions are under-girded with strong classical, jazz and hymnology structures.

Happily married since 1970 to Lesley, they parented five children-Rachel, Daniel, and triplets, Mark, Hannah and Sarah. Rachel became a doctor and Daniel a professional studio engineer. A great sports lover, Chris and the whole family share an avid support for the Aston Villa Football Club located in the midlands of England.

One of Chris's best songs is the prayerful plea to *"Fill The Place Lord With Your Glory"*.

The scriptural Hebrew word "kabod", translated "glory" means the "weight". This, therefore, speaks of the "worth" of something. For example we speak of "someone whose word carries weight". Chris' song subject is "the Glory of God" that is the "Worthiness of

God". The supplication song requests the Presence of God (in all the fullness of His attributes) in the specific place where the local church meets.

The glory-filled presence of God in the Old Testament was later defined as the "Shekinah" (or "indwelling"). Several New Testament references to the Shekinah Glory can be found. Historically, God's Glory was revealed both physically and spiritually, as is seen in the Christmas story of the shepherds on the hills of Bethlehem, "and the glory of the Lord shone around them". Also in Christ' prayer for His disciples where it refers to the "glory of the Father that Jesus gave to His disciples". As for the believing saints, glory culminates in the changing of their bodies to the likeness of their glorified Lord.

The Glory of God in local church assemblies is the exhibition of His divine attributes, the radiance of His presence. Chris says, *"My song is firstly, a prayer petitioning the Lord for His presence when His 'called out ones' meet as the local church. Secondly, concerning us as individuals, the Glory of God is the manifestation in ordinary believers of commendable godly qualities such as wisdom, righteousness, self-control, ability and such. It is good to know that this Glory of God is the destiny of all believers! Given by God, it is the work of the Holy Spirit, secured by the death of Christ. It accompanies salvation by Christ and is thus inherited by all believers!"*

Fill the place, Lord, with Your glory,
At this gathering of Your own;
Reign in sovereign grace and power
From Your praise-surrounded throne.

Fill the place, Lord, with Your glory,
At this gathering of Your own:
We exalt You, we adore You,
Thankful hearts now join as one.

You're the Christ, the King of glory,
Father's well-beloved son.
Fill the place, Lord, with your glory,
At this gathering of Your own.

Chris Bowater Copyright © 1983 Sovereign Lifestyle Music Ltd
P O Box 356 Leighton Buzzard Beds LU7 8WP
Used by permission

For His Name Is Exalted
David & Dale Garrett

*'But (He) made himself of no reputation, and took upon
him the form of a servant, and was made in the likeness of
men:*
*And being found in fashion as a man, he humbled himself,
and became obedient unto death, even the death of the cross.
Wherefore God also hath highly exalted him,
and given him a name which is above every name:
That at the name of Jesus every knee should bow,
of things in heaven, and things in earth, and things under
the earth;
And that every tongue should confess that Jesus Christ is Lord,
to the glory of God the Father.'*
(Philippians 2:7-11)

New Zealand's songwriting husband and wife duo, Dave and Dale
Garrett were early pioneers of the 'Scripture in Song' music style of
the late Sixties. Dave was born in Wellington, the capital city, the
second of eleven children. His father started as a carpenter by trade
but then managed a firm dealing with chemistry appliances. Dave's
early Christian influence came by way of his parents who he said
were strong fundamental evangelicals. Looking back to his youth,
he said *"Their faith was very real! That's something I realised as a
boy!"* Leaving school, Dave's early career was in the tea trade

traveling extensively to the poorer tea-producing countries. *"The trips"*, he said, *"opened my eyes to how poor people in the world lived!"*

Dave and Dale first became aware of each other at a Youth For Christ meeting in the North Island city of Auckland. Dave was performing and Dale was in the audience. Before that eventful meeting, they had worked together previously as singers. As he told me, Dave believed the timing of their second meeting was crucial in both their lives. *"I am sure it was the timing of God because when we did fall in love, it was right! Prior to that, it could have been a diversion for us!"* Later as husband and wife, the duo joined together to write gospel songs. *"Dale does the writing but I sometimes suggest to her themes, scriptures or ideas!...I also do a bit of spontaneous singing!"*

In 1968 the duo recorded some of their "scripture songs" and called them "Scriptures in Song". The concept (using scriptures verbatim) was in itself not a new one. Many times thoughout history, hymn and gospel song-writers used written Scripture as their base. When asked where the Garretts' concept came from Dale said, *"It was really just something the Lord dropped on us! Several years before we were praying for a musical way to express ourselves and communicate to people things that had more meat than the sort of popular 'Sweet Bye and Bye' type of song. We heard some of the first Scripture Songs and felt we should put them on record. That was the simple beginning!"* When the modest albums were released, the simple yet elegant songs were described as "anointed" by some people. When asked the reason for this perception, Dale replied, *"I guess we tried to respond to what the Holy Spirit said to us! If what one does is motivated by God, one can expect the Lord to bless it! That's the way it was! Neither of us were musicians, we were congregational singers rather than performing artists. At the same time, we become a demonstration to people in the area of praise and worship. We were able to use songs to teach in a prophetic sense and deliver something of God's Word to people! God's Word teaches that His Word will never return unto Him void. That is to say whenever the Word is proclaimed it will accomplish that purpose it was meant to do!*

A song is a tremendous way of communicating and of learning God's Word. As we sing something of truth, we feel like we are putting food into people who hear and learn. Just as Jesus said, 'Man does not live by bread alone but by every word that proceeds from the mouth of God'! The Word of God is food for all! As a result we try to ensure that the content of our songs is worth singing and learning!"

The popularity of the 'Scripture in Song' concept flowed over into most mainstream churches in the second half of the last Century laying the foundation of what became the worship chorus phenomenon. Song books to accompany the 'Scripture in Song' albums were produced. Many churches used them as a tool in their congregational worship. The result of the Scripture in Song concept was summed up by Dale. *"As we continue to listen to what the Holy Spirit is saying, we are able to put tools in the hands of God's people that are life-changing. We disciple people in using music prophetically. Later, they too can train and teach others. Whatever we're doing that is 'of God' will be multiplied!"*

The words in Philippians 2:7-11 have a poetic, even lyrical mannerism. Many scholars view them as an early Christian hymn, taken over and perhaps modified by the Apostle Paul. Whether so or not, the beautiful words nonetheless express his convictions. The passage addresses Christ's humiliation and exaltation, affirming that Jesus is fully God. The sum of Christ's qualities makes Him specifically God. Status and the privileges inevitably follow from being in very nature God. However, He did not consider that high position to be something He could not give up! He "emptied Himself" not by giving up deity, but by laying aside His glory and submitting to the humiliation of becoming a human being. Jesus was truly God and truly human. He was always submissive to the will of the Father. Not only was Jesus "like" a human being, but he also took on the actual outward characteristics of a human being and humbled Himself, obedient to death. *"The Cross",* said Dave, *"heightened Jesus' humiliation! He died as someone cursed! Crucifixion was the most degrading kind of execution that could be inflicted on a person. But today, as our praise chorus proclaims, He is exalted and possesses the Name above every name! God's intent was and is that all people everywhere should worship and serve Jesus as Lord. Ultimately all will acknowledge Him as Lord, whether willingly or not!"*

His glory is above the earth and heaven (Psalm 148:13)

Holy, holy, holy, Lord God Almighty, which was, and is, and is to come. (Revelation 4:8)

Freely, Freely
Carol Owens

'And as ye go, preach, saying, The kingdom of heaven is at hand.
Heal the sick, cleanse the lepers, raise the dead, cast out devils: freely ye have received, freely give.'
(Matthew 10: 7-8)

The song "Freely, Freely" from the "Come Together" musical speaks of the kind of charitableness encouraged and commanded by Christ and that pleases God.

On both sides of the Atlantic, 1972 saw a special innovation in gospel music led by Pat Boone. In the final quarter of the Millennium, it notably altered the traditional image of church use of contemporary Christian music in worship. "Freely, Freely" from the musical 'Come Together' is one of several Jimmy and Carol Owens' songs absorbed into the mainstream of hymnody that are still in use today. "Freely, Freely" was penned by Carol who was born on 30 October 1931.

Jimmy says, *"The seeds of the 'Come Together' were divinely sown in our lives. Along with Pat Boone, we were involved in the so called 'Jesus People' movement of the Seventies!"* An experienced choir conductor and music arranger (for movies, TV and audio recording) at the time, Jimmy and his wife, Carol with their two teenage children, daughter Jamie and son Buddy attended the 'Church on the Way' pastored by Jack Hayford. Jimmy first met Pat in 1966 and produced and arranged two of Pat's Christian albums in 1970 and 1971. It was while working on these that Jimmy invited Pat and his family to their church.

While the Owens were eating together at Jack Hayford's house after Sunday night church, Jack dropped a casual suggestion into the chat. *'Why don't you write a musical about our church?'* Jimmy nor Carol took the suggestion very seriously, but by the next morning they knew it was their next assignment from the Lord. It was to be a musical not 'about' the church, but setting forth the principles of ministry to be shared with other churches.

"Recognising this to be instructions from the Lord, we started work almost immediately. Gradually, we began to realise that 'Come Together' was a gift from God to the universal church!"

Jimmy and Pat worked together, Jimmy conducting the singers and Pat leading the worship. As the presentations began to spread to other parts of the USA, it became impossible for Pat and Jimmy to be present at all of them, so each local church provided its own musicians and worship leader. The impact of this innovative presentation made itself known in other parts of the world. At the height of severely damaging exposes of sex scandals involving some UK Government ministers, in the summer of 1973, the Owens were invited to England by Jean and Elmer Darnell to promote 'Come Together' in some 400 presentations, many in the largest halls and cathedrals. Local mass choirs, totalling thousands, sprang-up. It was a pivotal time in the church - the early days of the *'Jesus Movement'*, the *'Charismatic Movement'*, the *'House Church Movement'* and the *'Praise and Worship Movement'*. "Come Together" became vehicle a to help spread them all. At the time, the condition of the United Kingdom was spiritually and socially in crisis. Churches were often small and their relationships contentious. Socially, inflation, unemployment, and crippling strikes and riots were rampant. "Come Together" brought many diverse churches together for worship and ultimately gave new unity and strength to the nation. One of the most challenging and memorable songs in the musical was "Freely, Freely"

Without doubt, Pat Boone was 'Come Together''s initial, biggest drawing-card. But, like a snowball rolling down hill, news of its success began to circulate. The venues experienced crowds not seen for many years, including Belfast, Northern Ireland. Thirty years later, Carol still enthuses about the days. *"When we flew into Belfast, to present 'Come Together' the streets were full of barbed wire and armed men! Our auditorium had a boarded up window where a British soldier had been killed by a sniper a couple of days earlier and some of the warring factions had let us know they didn't like our message!"*

On the River Thames, opposite the Houses of Parliament, London's Westminster Central Hall, was packed to capacity the first night with over a thousand people *unable* to get in! Undaunted, the crowd outside nevertheless joined in with the spirit of 'Come Together' and held their own worship celebration, singing and praying in the falling rain!

To those who never attended a 'Come Together' presentation it is difficult to explain what it was, as Pat outlined. *"Some folks have likened it to Handel's 'Messiah'! It had its own Hallelujah Chorus perhaps the similarity is there!...Like the 'Messiah' in its day, the music is contemporary. But there the similarity ends as 'Come Together' seeks to involve the whole congregation in worship, splitting up into small prayer groups to pray for individuals!"* Most of the dialogue by Pat was mainly Scripture, though not all of it. There was an informality, freedom in worship without it becoming frivolous or sacrilegious, with a strong emphasis on keeping discipline. Many attendees found a new liberty in their style of worship that still carries on today. "Come Together" also promoted the use of contemporary songs as well as older hymns in church services! The highest focus of all was on "serving others" as the song reminded all.

God forgave my sin in Jesus' name,
I've been born again in Jesus' name;
And in Jesus' name I come to you
To share His love as He told me to.

He said: 'Freely, freely, you have received,
Freely, freely give;

Go in My name, and because you believe
Others will know that I live.'

God's Balladeer (The Ballad of Ira Sankey)
Roger Hill

'O give thanks unto the LORD; call upon his name:
make known his deeds among the people.
Sing unto him, sing psalms unto him:
talk ye of all his wondrous works.'
(Psalm 105:1-2)

English songwriter, Roger Hill also is a freelance columnist, record reviewer and musician. His articles appeared in 'Floodtide' and 'New Christian Media Magazine'. Resident in Beckenham, Kent, he is a member of Bromley Baptist Church.

For years, he says that he was fascinated by the achievements of the gospel singing soloist, Ira Sankey. Then he heard that country star, George Hamilton IV of Nashville, Tennessee was recording a tribute album and decided to pen a biographical ballad for George. Roger told me, *"The inspiring, heart warming story of Ira Sankey underlines what a comfort and joy gospel music can be! He believed passionately that whether in times of sunshine, or in times of storm, gospel music can stir and inspire the Christian's spirit, and act as a 'salt shaker' in society. Ira was the greatest Victorian pioneer of inspirational sacred music and perhaps the greatest of all time. Twentieth Century Christians never realised that much of their inherited gospel music came from Ira's dedicated efforts."*

Born in Bushey, Hertfordshire on the 24 November 1947, Roger Hill's earliest recollection of life was staring at a huge bath, answering to the name of Peter and living in an orphanage somewhere in Birmingham, England. At four years of age, he barely remembers being adopted by a new father, William Hill and thus being taken to his new home and family in the greenery of Farnborough, Kent. Roger tells me, *"The things I value most in life were taught to me by my new Father but some things took more time than others to sink in!"*

Roger developed an avid love of certain artistic disciplines including what he calls high brow music. Nowadays, he can hardly believe (and is tickled by the thought) that he was trained for St Paul's Cathedral School choir but failed the entry examination. A love for reading was another discipline that Roger says was ingrained into his personality. *"I was studiously taught by my Father to read aloud books like Charles Dickens' novels and the Greek Classics at about the young age of ten."*

A hard worker himself, the eager Father believed that the work ethic was essential for success and therefore taught his new son Roger not to be afraid of hard work. Later Roger developed a passion for many kinds of sports but especially the gentlemanly game of cricket and cycle racing.

Now in a church-going family, Roger was encouraged to go to church and taught to pray the Lord's Prayer.

"Yet learning all these things", Roger remembers, *"could not correct my bad behaviour, heal my constant illnesses and cure my emotional instability. My dysfunctional background left emotional scars on my personality that I realise now caused my Father and others a lot of pain. The problems deepened when my Father's first wife died and two years later he married again. This situation caused great resentment against my Father that lasted for a long time. I had an anger inside me that I could not control and I wanted to hurt people anyway I could either physically, emotionally or materially!"*

By the time Roger had reached his late teens, he had served a youth borstal sentence, been in London's notorious Wormwood Scrubs Prison and was well known by the local police for his anti-

social way of life. He said that his only relief from his problems was
to consume amphetamine pills.

Roger today finds the memory painful and yet he says there was
hope! *"The One who knows me best was not condemning me but
using some dear Christian saints to pray for me. Finally, just like
the Prodigal Son I came to my senses and turned to the Only Person
who could heal me, cure me and calm the raging anger inside me.
But the work God has done in my life took a long time and He used
some dear loving saints to correct and steer me on the right path.
I'm glad to say that the work of regeneration that God operates is
steadfast and eternal. I could never have cleansed, healed and put
myself right with God. Only Jesus could make it possible for me to
begin again. It is a miracle that God should love me and take time to
search for me. It's great to know that nowadays I can be of use to
Him where I live in south-east London. I still have to repent daily for
the bad thoughts, selfishness and such, but I know I can go to Jesus
any time and tell Him what is on my mind. and He will hear me!"*

*In history's rich vein of sacred singers came a soloist, faithful
and true.*

*He sang of God's deliverance and mercy, and of a land beyond
the blue!*

Born in 1840 was Ira, early he learned to sing of God's love,

*And many a cold heart was melted, strangely warmed by the
Heavenly Dove!*

*Raised on his parents 'homestead', he saw God's creation close
around.*

*There were cows to milk, barns to clean, Crops of vegetables in
the ground.*

*When Unionists and Confederates divided, they fought a violent
civil war.*

Soldier, Ira marched for the North, and sentry duty was his chore.

A Southern sniper aimed his rifle to put the singing sentry down.

But was captured by Ira's psalm and surrendered to the sound!

Ira's life was spared that starry night to sing to noble and low,

*Destined to influence England's Queen and presidents we
know!*

Always looking smart and groomed, in a tax office Ira earned his pay,

And after leaving the army, became a delegate for the YMCA.

At a prayer meeting God brought to Ira, preacher Moody, a partner so true.

Together, they sailed the oceans telling lost souls of life anew.

Many hymns co-penned by this tunesmith spanned the pages of history.

'There Were Ninety and Nine' safely 'Under His Wings' plus 'Faith Is The Victory!'

At the dawn of the twentieth century, still singing, the half has ne'er been told!

Then 'Til We Meet Again!' filled chapel rafters, God's balladeer was finally called home.

(Roger Hill © New Music Enterprises 1999
pauldavis@newmusic28.freeserve.co.uk / Used with permission)

God Be With You Till We Meet Again
Jeremiah Rankin & William Tomer

'Then we which are alive and remain shall be caught up together with them in the clouds, to meet the Lord in the air: and so shall we ever be with the Lord.
Wherefore comfort one another with these words.'
(1 Thessalonians 4:17-18)

The writer of this hymn, Dr. Jeremiah Rankin was born in Thornton, New Hampshire in 1828 and died in 1904. Educated at nearby Middlebury College, he then went on to study for the Christian ministry at Andover Theological Seminary and in 1855 was ordained into the Congregational Church and serving in several pastorates of New York, Vermont and Massachusetts. At the time this farewell hymn was written, Dr. Rankin was serving God as pastor of the First Congregational church, Washington DC, and it seems that the song was aptly written for no other reason than to be a Benediction hymn to be sung at the end of each service.

Jeremiah wrote the first verse using the line 'God Be With You' which he felt was of much more spiritual meaning than the usual 'good-bye'. He then sent the song (which at that time only contained one verse) to his friend William G. Tomer, organist at the Grace Methodist Episcopal Church. William was a veteran of the American Civil War serving with the 153rd Pennsylvania Infantry. After the war, he spent 20 years as a government employee in Washington DC whilst also serving as music director at the Grace Methodist

Episcopal Church. Taking Jeremiah's first verse, he put the words to music and sent it back to him. William then added a further seven verses and chorus. The song first appeared in print in the Gospel Bells hymnbook compiled in 1883. It was popularised by Ira Sankey who used it extensively in his numerous evangelistic campaigns.

One hundred years later, opportunities to sing abroad started to increase for the Blackwood Brothers Quartet. During the Seventies, at the height of the Cold War, the relationship of the West with the communist Soviet block was decidedly frosty, but the Quartet of James Blackwood, Cecil Blackwood, Ken Turner, and Pat Hoffmaster decided on the dangerous move to take the gospel to Russia. American gospel music artistes had never been given even a passing whiff of an invitation into the bastions of socialist experimentation behind the fearful 'Iron Curtain'. Things were primitive, restricted and sometimes dangerous in 1974! Everyday life for everyday folk was undoubtedly tough.

It was a crisp, dry, sunny morning and it was their first encounter with Cold War politics. Years later, Cecil reminisced to me accordingly about the great Soviet adventure. *'On the Russian border, we advised everyone that we should prudently declare ourselves to be 'folk-singing tourists' rather than 'gospel-singing evangelists'. There was no need to unduly stir antagonism among the guards of this atheistic State!'* Cecil was the first to be quizzed at the border post but, to his great relief, he was the first to be admitted. After him came James. Then calamity struck. 'Ken Turner let it slip! He admitted that he was a gospel singer!...The fearsome guards started to inspect all the American baggage with gleeful zeal. Sure enough, they discovered a large consignment of Bibles! Cecil was duly arrested with cold efficiency and thrown into a dismal cell. Photos were taken of the shaken prisoner with the contraband goods. The aggressive questioning was intimidating and threats were made. The uncomfortable imprisonment lasted for hours, as Cecil fearfully contemplated what would be his fate at the hands of such a cruel State system. The tempter actively tried to sow seeds of despair and fear, as his thoughts raced. Outside, the tour party prayed earnestly and tearfully, pleading for Cecil's divine protection and release. Quicker than anyone had dared hope, the prison door was swung open. A shaken, ruffled Cecil was returned to his friends who greeted him with sighs and cries of relieved hallelujahs.

Reaching their St. Petersburg hotel destination after a good rest, Cecil asked their Russian guide if she would guide the Blackwood Brothers to the Church called *'The Temple Of The Gospel'* where they planned to sing. She refused, worried and frightened about the secret police watching the Americans' movements carefully. In desperation, Cecil phoned the Church. After several voices, none of whom spoke English, he managed to reach an associate pastor. Sergei Nikolaev spoke pigeon-English through a thick Russian accent.

'Come on over!...Brother Cecil, we're waiting for you all!...Welcome to Russia in the name of our dear Saviour!'

It took ten taxi-cabs to ferry the whole party from the hotel through miles and miles of poor, bleak, grey streets to the unimposing, old, grey, soot-dyed building. Although language communications were difficult, the warm Christian greetings given to the party in the church courtyard were heart-felt. Tears, smiles and hugs said it all! The hosts warmly and emotionally embraced their visitors. Then the gifts including the prized Bibles were distributed followed by an impromptu worship-time as the Christians from East and West praised God together in unison. They gathered in lines of rough-hewn, narrow pews that quickly filled with work-weary people dressed in layers of hand-patched clothes.

Nervously at first, but gaining conviction, James grinned and greeted the smiling congregation. *'We are the Blackwood Brothers from Memphis, Tennessee....We are fellow Christians!...We are your brothers!...We bring greetings from your fellow Christians in America!'* Then to the Blackwoods utter amazement, as tears swelled in their eyes, the poorly-dressed Russian people in the congregation jumped to their feet and waved their hankies. Loud *'hallelujah'* cries of delight echoed around the building in Russian! *'Thank you!...Thank you, Jesus!...Hallelujah!...Praise the Lord!'*

Later in the church basement, the Russian Christians sacrificially fed their American guests with home-baked cakes and cookies plus pop to drink. What the affluent visitors had not realised back then was that the ordinary citizens of that stark Communist State were enduring severe food shortages. The common people were experiencing great difficulty in obtaining even the basic necessities of life.

The *'thank yous'* over, it was time to part. Spontaneously the Russians embraced their emotional guests for the last time then bubbled into-'God Be With You Till We Meet Again'! It was the final good-bye gesture to their American brethren. Most lost their composure and many wept openly. As Cecil recalled life-long friendships were forged that day.

God be with you till we meet again!
By His counsels guide, uphold you,
With His sheep securely fold you:
God be with you till we meet again!

Till we meet, till we meet,
Till we meet at Jesus' feet
Till we meet, till we meet,
God be with you till we meet again!

God be with you till we meet again!
'Neath His wings protecting hide you,
Daily manna still provide you;
God be with you till we meet again!

God be with you till we meet again!
When life's perils thick confound you,
Put His arms unfailing round you
God be with you till we meet again!

God be with you till we meet again!
Keep love's banner floating o'er you,
Smite death's threatening wave before you:
God be with you till we meet again!

Jeremiah Eames Rankin 1828-1904

Great Is Thy Faithfulness
Thomas Chisholm & William Runyan

*'It is of the LORD'S mercies that we are not consumed,
because his compassions fail not.
They are new every morning: great is thy faithfulness.
The LORD is my portion, saith my soul; therefore will I hope
in him.'
(Lamentations 3:22-24)*

The author of this beloved song-'Great Is Thy Faithfulness'- was Thomas Obadiah Chisholm who was born in Franklin, Kentucky in 1866 and died in 1960. He chose teaching as a career despite receiving no high school or other specialised training for the job. As was often the case in those days, he started to teach in the same little country school where he himself was educated. He then became editor of the local newspaper- 'Franklin Favourite'- when he was only 21 years old. Six years later was his dramatic Christian conversion during a revival meeting in his hometown held by Dr. H. C. Morrison. The preacher later invited Thomas to become office editor and business manager of his 'Pentecostal Herald' newspaper in Louisville, Kentucky.

Sensing the divine call to the Christian ministry, he became an ordained Methodist minister. However, because of ill health, he left the ministry becoming instead a life insurance agent. During this time he also began writing sacred poems. Writing more than 1200 in his lifetime, hundreds of them appeared in print in religious publications. Some were also used as hymn texts, the most renowned one of which was 'Great is Thy Faithfulness' based on Lamentations 3:22-24.

The poem was sent by Thomas in 1923 to the Methodist evangelist, Rev. William Marion Runyan (1870-1957) in Baldwin, Kansas. Subsequently, William and Thomas co-wrote about twenty-five hymns together. Such was the impact of the words of the 'Great Is Thy Faithfulness' poem, William prayed that God would give him a tune that would perfectly reflect the message. The result was the beautiful melody, 'Faithfulness'. However, the hymn did not make any impact on the Christian world for several years until the then president of the famed Moody Bible Institute, Dr. Houghton, began to use it extensively. It soon became a favourite of the students, almost an unofficial theme song of the Institute, thus enlarging its popularity considerably. Then the song was popularised worldwide by George Beverly Shea in the Billy Graham missions.

In January 2001, 56 years after the end of World War II in Europe, the United Kingdom under Prime Minister Tony Blair (along with nations) instituted an annual memorial. Called Holocaust Day, it was to remind current and future generations of the genocide brought against the Jewish people in the Thirties and Forties during the reign of Hitler and his Nazi Party. The horrific Jewish tragedy was truly a cause for great lamentations.

The prophet Jeremiah was an eyewitness to the divine judgement on Jerusalem in 586 BC and so vividly portrays the event. The book of Lamentations poignantly describes the overwhelming sense of loss that accompanied the destruction of the city, temple and ritual as well as the exile of Judah's inhabitants. 'Great Is Thy Faithfulness' comes directly from this horrific event. The entire book tells of a Holocaust Day in poetic form. Lamentations is not the only Old Testament book that contains individual or community laments. However, it is the only book that consists solely of laments. Orthodox Jews customarily read it aloud in its entirety on the ninth day of Ab, the traditional date of the destruction of Solomon's temple in 586 as well as the date of the destruction of Herod's temple in A.D. 70. Many also read it each week at the Western Wall (known also as the

"Wailing Wall") in the Old City of Jerusalem. The horrors of 586 BC are not forgotten including the wholesale devastation and slaughter engulfing kings, princes, elders, priests, prophets and commoners alike. Starving mothers were reduced to cannibalism, the flower of Judah's citizenry was dragged off into ignominious exile and the nation's elaborate system of ceremony and worship brought to an end. Yet ultimately of far greater significance, the author of Lamentations understood clearly that amid the tragedy, in the middle of the book, the theology of Lamentations reaches its apex as it focuses on the goodness of God. He is the Lord of hope, of love, of faithfulness, of salvation. In spite of all evidence to the contrary, 'His compassions never fail. They are new every morning; great is Your faithfulness!'

Great is Thy faithfulness, O God my Father,
There is no shadow of turning with Thee;
Thou changest not, Thy compassions, they fail not;
As Thou hast been Thou forever wilt be.

Great is Thy faithfulness!
Great is Thy faithfulness!
Morning by morning new mercies I see;
All I have needed Thy hand hath provided,
Great is Thy faithfulness, Lord, unto me!

Thomas O. Chisholm (1866–1960) William M. Runyan (1870–1957)
Copyright © 1951 Hope Publishing Co/Adm. by CopyCare,
PO Box 77, Hailsham, BN27 3EF, England.)
music@copycare.com/ Used by permission

He Is Exalted
Twila Paris

'Sing praises to God, sing praises: sing praises unto our King, sing praises.
For God is the King of all the earth: sing ye praises with understanding.
God reigneth over the heathen: God sitteth upon the throne of his holiness.
The princes of the people are gathered together, even the people of the God of Abraham:
for the shields of the earth belong unto God: he is greatly exalted!'
(Psalm 47:6-9)

In Psalm 33 we are encouraged to 'play skilfully and shout for joy'. David was one who followed this advice. Not only did David write lyrics that still soar after thousands of years. He was also a gifted musician who played his instrument as worship to the Lord. And his music lifted the spirits and calmed the hearts of those around him. Twila Paris-the writer of "He Is Exalted"- says, *"Using David as our example, I hope and pray that my music will inspire worship in your spirit, lighten your heart and minister peace."*

Twila Paris' healthy Christian heritage was the clue to her strong motivation. *"My dear Father was an evangelist and pastor, one of a family of ministers!"* After Twila was born on 28 December 1958, it soon became apparent that this fair little lass was endowed with an admirable singing voice. Even from a very early age the capability was gradually perfected. In her cute "Shirley Temple" dresses, she loved to perform for audiences no matter how small. At the age of four years, bolstered by her Father, she charmingly recorded an album for children entitled "Little Twila Paris"! When she was seven, the family moved to Springdale, Arkansas where her father pastored a church. It was a trying time for the youngster as she sought to make new friends. She found consolation in music, being taught to play the piano by her Father. An accomplished pianist and composer, himself, he wrote what were (in his day) contemporary Christian songs.

Her Father was a great discipling influence in Twila's life and music. *"My father always encouraged me! I questioned him about the future. The questions I had about my life involved God's will, and whether I should be singing. Questions never involved whether or not I could do it! My Dad had always told me I could and I believed him!"*

Entering high school, teenager Twila studied computer programming. But during one semester, she swapped from a maths class to a chorus class. The notion of a musical career began to constitute in her adolescent mind. By this time, her Father was now director of the Springdale base of the very active "Youth With A Mission" organisation. As its name implies, YWAM evangelically concentrated on discipling and the sending out of mainly young people into the mission field. So subsequent to her graduation, Twila resolved to join a YWAM training school touring with a music and drama team. Her solo performing endeavours proved to be very acceptable to audiences wherever she went. People kept questioning her asking whether she had recorded any of her songs and where could they purchase them. With such a demand building, a confidant suggested she record a custom album (one paid for and distributed by the artist).

Adventurously, this she did! When the finished Christian recording was dispatched to a record company, executives quickly recognised Twila's qualitative potential so she was duly signed up.

Soon she was one of the record company's top-selling contemporary Christian artists.

Twila continued to minister with YWAM and not surprisingly perhaps, her songs mirrored her deep commitment to her Lord. Her Christian priorities majored on worship, praise and the importance of missions. Twila said, *"Maintaining Christ Jesus at the heart of my musical message was always my top priority...The Church too should be serious in its commitment to keep Christ and His objectives in their sight! His purposes should always be our ultimate goal!...The bottom line is not WHAT we do, but WHY we do it! It's very important to retain the right motivation!"*

Coming to terms with that belief was, she says, the turning point in the musical career of this attractive singer and composer of contemporary Christian music. With her winsome looks and musical quality she could easily have been engulfed in showbiz pursuits. But, as she explained, she remained jealous of her "heavenly calling". *"I really felt there was a call on my life from God, to be used in music. I think, in one sense, that's why I wanted a music career so badly! But somehow, in between, I let my own personal ambitions creep in. Then I had to determine what was from God and what was from me! I had to come to the place where I was able to say, 'God, if You don't want me to have a career in music, that's okay!...I want to do with my life whatever will serve You and Your kingdom."*

A central theme is shared by both Twila Paris' devotional song and the poem of Psalm 47. It portrays the liturgical "ascension of God to the temple" represented by the processional bearing of the Ark of the Covenant into the Temple of old Jerusalem. The Ark was religiously symbolic of "God's throne" while the "Temple" was the earthly symbol of His heavenly palace. The ancient public event was accompanied by shouts of joy from the people and the sounding of trumpets. The blowing of the ram's horn prophetically announced the presence of God as King. The Psalm was the liturgical enthronement of God as "world ruler, the King of all the earth"! Twila's song and the Psalm pictures Him seated on His holy throne, enthroned in the Most Holy Place of the temple. It describes Him taking the reins of world rule into His safe hands. This theme is frequently echoed in the Book of Revelation as all nations acknowledge the God of Israel to be the Great King, anticipated as the final accomplishment of God's rule. Thus the promises to Abraham and his descendants will be fulfilled.

> *He is exalted, the King is exalted on high;*
> *I will praise Him.*
> *He is exalted, for ever exalted*
> *And I will praise His name!*
> *He is the Lord; for ever his truth shall reign,*
> *Heaven and earth rejoice in His holy Name.*
> *He is exalted, the King is exalted on high.*

He's Alive!
Don Francisco

'Jesus said ... I am the resurrection, and the life:
he that believeth in me, though he were dead, yet shall he
live:
And whosoever liveth and believeth in me shall never die!'
(John 11:25-26)

"He's Alive" is a wonderful story song of the first Easter's Resurrection Morning seen through the eyes of the Apostle Peter. The author-Don Francisco made a swift rise to worldwide fame through the medium of his unique singing. Initially under the production genius of Gary S. Paxton, his song-writing style soon gathered attention. His hit songs were recorded by the likes of Johnny Cash, Dolly Parton, Wanda Jackson, Jerry Arhelger, The Gaithers, and Doug Oldham...to name a few!

"He's Alive" proved to be so popular that it won a Dove Award for the Song Of The Year. As he recalled, Don was thrilled when asked by Johnny Cash to attend Johnny's recording of the song. *"In the studio when Johnny was recording I witnessed something terrible happen! One of the sound engineers slipped accidentally and hit the 'record button' with his elbow erasing a second and a half from all 24 tracks right in the middle of 'He's alive'! That's the worst thing that could happen at a session!...They'd put in, prior to this incident, approximately one hundred man-hours into the song, not to mention tape and studio time... I got to find out what Johnny was made of at that time. A lesser man would have just completely lost his temper at such foolishness but Johnny just gritted his teeth, walked outside and came back about ten minutes later praising the Lord! Evidently, he took the victory over the situation and got back to work on it! I really liked the result and enjoyed hearing him sing 'He's Alive'. Johnny's sincerity really comes through and that's what I care about most! When I hear someone sing I like to know they really mean it!"*

Don's well cultured, bearded appearance and exotic name conjures up nostalgic memories of 'Zorro' adventures or such! His singing career evoked considerable public acclaim since he first nervously opened up for the popular Bill and Gloria Gaither concerts in the Eighties. Audiences discovered his poetic folk style to be challenging, clean-cut and captivating. Surprisingly, Don Francisco is his real name, not a stage name. He told me, *"It seems from what we can tell our ancestors went to the States about 200 years ago from Portugal. That's where the name came from!"*

A gospel-storyteller-in-song of the first order, he well deserved the prime exposure afforded to him. His sound was contemporary country-folk-rock, his inspirational songs, unique with a sharp-cutting edge making them distinctively his. This unique storyteller-in-song possessed the rare ability to match a complex tale to a melody line while simultaneously striking the listener a cutting-message stroke.

Theologically, Don considered it more effective to paint a picture-in-song rather than point a finger as a means of touching people! His treasured aim, he says, is the objective of spreading the gospel. He has held this conviction since the age of twenty eight. At the time, he experienced the most potent spiritual episode of his life. As a mature adult, it revolutionised his direction. Subsequently, to him it was natural that he use his God-given music to communicate the reality of his spiritual experience.

Raised in Louisville, Kentucky, his father was a preacher and a teacher of the Old Testament scriptures at the Southern Baptist Theological Seminary. Don remembers nostalgically the heart warming gospel singing duets that his parents sang in church. His formative younger years were spent in various church choirs. It seemed that he had a natural aptitude for music and was a good communicator. He was not, however, without any inhibitions. As he explained, *"When I was a kid I stuttered so badly I could hardly talk but singing was a way whereby I could communicate with people!"*

Young Don's musical career began with the purchase of his first guitar from the winnings of a blackjack game held during the time he should have been in Sunday School! The prize was 24 dollars which for a kid in 1960 was a fortune! It allowed him to buy and experiment on his first guitar, developing a love affair with the instrument, practising until his fingers bled. Not unusually, he hit the rebellious stage of his life at about the age of fourteen. All through high school and college, he sought "intellectual solutions" through studying religion, philosophy and psychology. In 1968, he experimented with drugs leading to "an education in sin and the ways of the world" on the streets of Los Angeles and San Francisco. He gained employment in a recording studio whilst singing in night clubs in the evenings. His blooming musical talent took him to sunny California. By 1969 he determined to pursue a music career, writing, singing and playing the guitar seriously. The songs written at this time showed his pain and confusion. Deep inside, he knew he was running from the Lord! After some success as a writer on the West coast, he moved back to the South. Forming his own band, he played lead guitar and sang back-up for several Nashville recording artists. Meanwhile meditating and doing yoga, he still sought that elusive inner peace! In 1974, at the age of 28, he became increasingly disillusioned with eastern philosophy. Realising he had tried everything, he came to the place where he didn't know where to turn to next! Giving the band he was playing in two weeks notice, he turned his back on that part of his life and headed back home to Decatur, Georgia. *"At this point I heard the Lord speak to me in an almost audible voice saying, 'I am Jesus, and I am alive in your heart. Read My Word and do it!'"*

There followed a period of intensive spiritual and physical housecleaning, deep studying of the Word and a reconstruction of a broken marriage. He then dedicated his life to a career in Christian music. His first album was released early in 1976 entitled "Brother of the Son". He summed up his ministry thus: '*I try to follow the leading of the Spirit in presenting the Word of God in contemporary language and song. The format consists of my own songs, older hymns and a few songs of others, interspersed with personal testimony and teaching from the word. My purpose is to bring those who do not know the Lord to a saving knowledge of Jesus Christ and to help Christians to worship and draw closer to Jesus.*'

Directness and clarity in his poetic lyrics were qualities that he tried to achieve from day one! He grew up in what he says was a "whole lot of Christian clichés"! He was determined not to fall into the same trap. Being clear and direct on stage, it was sometimes said that Don was somewhat too opinionated! Yet he says that he seldom found that people reacted badly to his criticism in song! He says jokingly, "*Most of the time they think I'm criticising other people rather than talking directly to them! Actually, I feel very uncomfortable every time I sing some songs because I don't always live up to the questions that the songs ask! I don't think there is anyone who does!!*"

And many other signs truly did Jesus in the presence of his disciples, which are not written in this book:
But these are written, that ye might believe that Jesus is the Christ, the Son of God; and that believing ye might have life through his name.
(John 20:30-31)

He's Everything To Me
Ralph Carmichael

'But what things were gain to me, those I counted loss for Christ.
Yea doubtless, and I count all things but loss for the excellency of the knowledge of Christ Jesus my Lord: for whom I have suffered the loss of all things, and do count them but dung, that I may win Christ,
And be found in him, not having mine own righteousness, which is of the law, but that which is through the faith of Christ, the righteousness which is of God by faith:'
(Philippians 3:7-9)

Songwriter, choir conductor and music publicist, Ralph Carmichael was born in Quincy, Illinois on 27 May 1927. A keen musician from a very young age, Ralph loved the old hymns and songs sung in his father's church. He began to eagerly study the violin at the tender age of four. Whilst studying at the Southern California College, Costa Mesa, Ralph became the church director of music at Calvary Assembly, Inglewood, California and directed a TV programme, 'The Campus Christian Hour,' utilising the musical skills of students. The popular programme eventually won him an Emmy Award. Ralph became a much sought-after orchestrator and record producer with diverse and august names as Frank Sinatra, Nat King Cole, Pat Boone, Tex Ritter, George Beverly Shea and

Jimmie Durante among his many credits. But perhaps, the moustached Ralph Carmichael is best known worldwide throughout the second half of the Twentieth Century for his musical scores of several Billy Graham Christian films. The movies featured several big musical names and Hollywood Christian actors including Redd Harper, Cindy Walker, Ethel Waters, Pat Boone, Dick Jones and Joan Winmill. His film credits include 'For Pete's Sake' the movie in which 'He's Everything To Me' was first featured. Other movies with Ralph Carmichael scores included 'The Restless Ones', 'The Shadow Of The Boomerang', 'The Cross and the Switchblade' and 'His Land' which remarkably featured England's Sir Cliff Richard and Cliff Barrows singing 'He's Everything To Me' in duet. Based in the Holy Land, it was a musical travelogue to the places of great Biblical significance.

Ralph says, *'My "He's Everything To Me" song is Christian music with lyrics that I wanted kids to relate to! I wanted it to be their kind of music with grammar, sentence structure and a situation to say geared to them. One day I had to ask myself if, as a composer of Christian music, I was saying anything. Was I communicating with the high school and college generations? I had to face the fact that many kids were calling me old fashioned. Their preference was the sounds of the Top 40. "He's Everything To Me" is still truth although sung to a beat, a tune that the new generation won't reject!'*

Ralph's 'He's Everything To Me' was based on the Apostle Paul's personal testimony of Philippians 3:7-9 that is a model for every believer in every generation. His personal testimony shines through his words in this one of his most significant autobiographical sections in his letters. Paul says that the true, inner meaning of Faith is realised only in believers who worship God with genuine spiritual worship and who glory in Christ as their Saviour rather than trusting in their own human qualifications, religious or otherwise.

In one way or other in the Apostle Paul's eyes, everyone is a 'boaster' either in Christ or in oneself that is in the flesh (weak human nature). Although the term 'flesh' in Paul's letters often refers to sinful human nature, it speaks here in Philippians 3 of the frailty of human nature. He says that it is not worthy of our confidence as it cannot save!

Paul's pre-Christian confidence was rooted in his outstanding Jewish pedigree, privileges and attainments.

He was born a Jew of the tribe of Benjamin and was not a proselyte. His Jewish roots were deep and unambiguous. He called himself a 'Hebrew of Hebrews' and in language, attitudes and life-style was a Pharisee. He said that his legalistic righteousness (righteousness produced by using the law as an attempt to merit God's approval and blessing) was faultless. In terms of legalistic standards of scrupulous external conformity to the law, he was beyond reproach.

Ralph's song expresses the Apostle Paul's confidence in Christ, a great reversal in Paul's thinking. It began on the road to Damascus when he changed from being 'self-centred' to being 'Christ-centred'! From then, he said that knowing Christ Jesus was not merely a knowledge of facts but a knowledge gained through experience that, in its surpassing greatness, transformed his entire person. His words spell this out: what Paul now had as a Christian was not merely preferable or a better alternative but in contrast, his former way of life was worthless and despicable. Union with Christ was not simply an experience in the past but a present, continuing relationship. 'Knowing Christ', he said, was not merely factual but included the experience of the power of His resurrection, of fellowship in His sufferings and of being like Him in His death. Moreover, believers already share positionally in Christ's death and resurrection. No wonder Ralph Carmichael was so excited when he wrote 'He's Everything To Me'!

For to me to live is Christ, and to die is gain.
Philippians 1:21

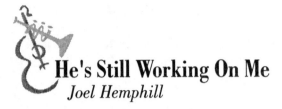

He's Still Working On Me
Joel Hemphill

*'And God saw every thing that he had made, and, behold,
it was very good.
And the evening and the morning were the sixth day.
Thus the heavens and the earth were finished, and all the
host of them.
And on the seventh day God ended his work which he had
made; and he rested on the seventh day from all his work
which he had made.
And God blessed the seventh day, and sanctified it:
because that in it he had rested from all his work which
God created and made.'
(Genesis 1:31-2:3)*

Over the past forty years, the name of Hemphill become established
as one of the most recognised names in the world of country gospel
music. Powerful family performers, they will be leaving a wonderful
legacy of classic gospel songs bearing the name of Hemphill to
subsequent generations. Life for everyone is made up of sunshine
and rain and the Hemphills are no exception to the rule. Many of
their moving songs like "He's Still Working on Me" have been written
as a result of dire circumstances in their personal lives. From their
experiences over the years came outstanding songs from Joel's pen
that have been recorded by a host of quality country and gospel acts
down including Hank Snow, The Gaithers and Wanda Jackson.

Initially, Joel Hemphill pastored a church in Bastrop, Louisiana from 1961 to 1971. With his wife LaBreeska they launched into their *country gospel music* career in 1972 as an evangelistic preaching and singing team. Moving to Nashville, it soon became more than just the duo with the addition of their children, Joey, Trent, and Candy. The family soon became one of the foremost groups in gospel music, famous for the talent of their personnel and quality of material, most of it written by Joel. From time to time, Joel, a quality preacher as well as an outstanding singer/songwriter, held pastorates in various churches.

They have received six Dove Awards and Joel was nominated ten times by the Gospel Music Association as song writer of the year. During his long career, Joel has penned more than three hundred songs including "He's Still Working on Me", "Master of the Wind", "Let's Have A Revival" and others.

By 1990, their grown-up children decided to pursue their own personal careers and Joel and LaBreeska were back to being *the duo* they started out as. But just as they were beginning their career all over again, tragedy struck when Joel was diagnosed as having cancer. The surgery proved to be successful, but was followed by severe clinical depression, rendering him totally disabled for over two years, forcing him to give up his normal life and career.

But LaBreeska's strong faith in God and the prayers of many of their friends kept them going.

Then on 8 November 1992, Joel was being prayed for at church by his pastor. As the pastor prayed Joel was suddenly healed. Even Joel's own doctor admitted that it was a miracle saying *"Prayer lifted his depression"*. Renewed in both body and spirit, Joel and LaBreeska took up their career again with a new passion and vigour in everything they do.

Joel says, *"Reading one day in Philippians 1:6, I saw that the Apostle Paul was speaking of God's work in a believer's life. Paul was confident, not only of what God has done FOR the believer in forgiving his sins, but also of what He has done IN them. Taking up this theme, I sat down and wrote this encouraging song, "He's Still Working On Me". The lyrics speak of God's total work and activity in saving us as Christians. It starts at the point of our rebirth but is fulfilled on the Day of Christ Jesus. At His return is when that salvation will be brought to completion. It is God who initiated our salvation and who continues it and who will one day bring it to its consummation. In other words, He's still working on us!"*

Being confident of this very thing,
that he which hath begun a good work in you
will perform it until the day of Jesus Christ: (Philippians 1:6)

His Name Is Wonderful
Audrey Mieir

'For unto us a child is born, unto us a son is given:
and the government shall be upon his shoulder:
and his name shall be called Wonderful,
Counseller, The mighty God, The everlasting Father, The
Prince of Peace.
Of the increase of his government and peace there shall be
no end, upon the throne of David, and upon his kingdom,
to order it, and to establish it with judgment and with
justice from henceforth even for ever.
The zeal of the LORD of hosts will perform this.'
(Isaiah 9:6-7)

Born on 12 May 1916 in Leechburg, Pennsylvania, Audrey Mae
Mieir's parents were Dow C. and Marie Elizabeth (Dorsey) Wagner.
A quick learner, the smiling round-faced Audrey was educated at
the L.I.F.E. Bible College. Just out of her teens, she fell madly in
love and married Charles B. Mieir in 1936. Inspired by her deep
faith, a year later, she was ordained into the gospel ministry of the
International Church of the Foursquare Gospel. Soon she was
actively using her musical and poetic skills in the ongoing cause
of Christ. From 1937-45 she was an evangelistic pianist on the
radio and on personal appearances. From 1946-58 she conducted
and organised several spirited choirs and the following year
founded the Mieir Choir Clinic in Hollywood. By now a successful

composer, pianist and choir clinician, she became very well known. She caught the eye of Hal Spencer of California's Manna Music Publications.

Many years had passed since she first started to write songs at the age of sixteen years of age. Inspired by the prophet Isaiah's foretelling of the birth of Christ, Audrey Mae Mieir penned "His Name is Wonderful" at Christmas time. Now an adult, she was actively involved in the family Christmas celebrations of her little Bethel Union Church in Duarte of greater Los Angeles, California where her brother-in-law-Dr. Luther Mieir pastored. The joyous Christmas presentation engaged the old and the young. The Virgin Mary was played appropriately by a pretty but nervous teenage girl who blushed at her central role. The angels were played by some playful young boys whose enthusiastic zeal was difficult to control and the aroma of sweet pine filled the decorated sanctuary. Audrey said, *"The atmosphere was so highly charged, I could almost sense the presence of God's angels!"* The organist played soft dreamy Christmas carols in the background while enthralled children sat quietly watching the amateur performances of their nervous peers. Older folks surreptitiously wiped tears from their watery eyes remembering nostalgic similar days of times gone by and captured by little Kodak box cameras. Paternally and deliberately, the pastor slowly rose from his platform preacher's chair. Extending his hands heavenward, he movingly declared, *"His Name is Wonderful!...His Name is Wonderful!...His Name is Wonderful!"*

An artistic songwriter to the core-Audrey's mind was stirred to poetic inspiration as she thought, *"Oh my, what a great theme for a worship song!!"* So not to forget, quickly, she roughly pencilled the title in the back page of her well-thumbed Bible. *"God",* she pondered, *"has something new that He wants said in those familiar words!"* Even before the moving service ended, praise-filled lyrics were starting to crystallise in her grey matter. Later that day, gathering the young people around the upright piano, she sang the new song immediately. No one there could ever have guessed that within only a few years her song-"His Name is Wonderful!"-would traverse the globe and be recorded by a host of top-class recording artistes such as the Anita Kerr Singers on RCA Victor.

Audrey's lyrics were a paraphrase of the prophet Isaiah's poetic prediction of Isaiah 9 referring to a royal son, a son of David, a great God of many "wonderful" attributes. Unlike His other name-'Immanuel', these four prophetically-given titles (the four throne names given of the Messiah) were not like normal Old Testament personal names. 'Counseller' points to the Messiah as a King who determines upon and carries out a programme of action. As the 'Wonderful Counseller', the coming Son of David carries out a royal programme that causes all the world to marvel! His divine power as a warrior is also stressed. As the 'Everlasting Father', He will be an enduring, compassionate Provider and Protector and as the 'Prince of Peace', His rule will bring wholeness and well-being to individuals and to society! No wonder Audrey declared that "His Name is Wonderful". Indeed, she lists His wonders also as He is the Mighty King, Master of Everything, the Great Shepherd, The Rock of all Ages and the Almighty God!

His name is Wonderful,
His name is Wonderful,
His name is Wonderful,
Jesus my Lord.
He is the mighty King,
Master of everything,
His name is Wonderful,
Jesus my Lord.

He's the great Shepherd,
The Rock of all ages,
Almighty God is He.
Bow down before Him,
Love and adore Him,
His name is Wonderful,
Jesus my Lord.

How Great Thou Art
Stuart K. Hine

> *'Let us come before his presence with thanksgiving,*
> *and make a joyful noise unto him with psalms.*
> *For the LORD is a great God, and a great King above all*
> *gods.*
> *In his hand are the deep places of the earth: the strength of*
> *the hills is his also.*
> *The sea is his, and he made it: and his hands formed the dry*
> *land.*
> *O come, let us worship and bow down: let us kneel before the*
> *LORD our maker.*
> *For he is our God; and we are the people of his pasture, and*
> *the sheep of his hand.'*
> *(Psalm 95:2-7)*

The melody of "How Great Thou Art" is unique, its lyrics majestic and poetically powerful in the high note of praise which they raise, perhaps the most popular modern hymn ever written. One hesitates, however, to call it modern because although it is relatively new to British and American ears, the truly impressive contemporary hymn received its popular form through three countries and three translators!

During the Billy Graham London Crusade in Harringey Arena in 1954, the well known soloist George Beverly Shea, whilst walking down Oxford street bumped into Andrew Grey, a friend who worked for the London publishing firm, Pickering and Inglis Ltd. As they chatted, the friend reached into his briefcase and pulled out two little four-page leaflets on which were printed what he described as a "new hymn". It was handed to Mr. Shea with the suggestion that he use it at Harringey. He thanked the friend but did not really examine the new contents very closely because contributions of that kind were often given to him. The other copy of the leaflet was given to Billy Graham Crusade songleader, Cliff Barrows. However the pace was far too hectic in those months of 1954 to consider a new arrangement and rehearsal in London. So the song was packed away. It was not until two or three months later, after Cliff and Bev returned to the USA that Bev came across the notes again. Sitting down at the piano he played it and sang it through. It was beautiful. He could barely wait to do it in a Crusade and mentioned "How Great Thou Art" to Cliff the next time they were together. Cliff agreed with Bev's enthusiasm about the song and handed copies to crusade pianist-Tedd Smith and organist-Paul Mickelson to work on arrangements together. The song had its debut performance at the Maple Leaf Garden Arena in Toronto, Canada in 1955. Bev remembers, *"The response was unbelievable! 'How Great Thou Art' was thereafter appreciated by every audience after its exposure in regular Crusades and on Billy Graham's 'Hour of Decision' radio broadcasts."*

This beautiful hymn, under its original title of "O Store Gud" (O Great God) started its life in Sweden in 1886. It was originally written as a poem by Rev. Carl Boberg, a well known preacher and religious editor, who also served for fifteen years as a senator in the Swedish Parliament. Added to the poem was a tune from an old, familiar Swedish folksong.

A German version 'Wie Gross Bist Du' was translated from the original Swedish by Manfred Von Glehn, an Estonian, in 1907 and five years later in 1912, Rev. Ivan S. Prokhanoff, who was known as the 'Martin Luther of Modern Russia' translated it into from German into Russian and published it in St. Petersburg. It was included in a collection of hymns entitled "Cymbals - A Collection Of Spiritual

Songs Translated From Various Languages". The unusual and wordy title of the book suggests the compiler took it from Psalm 150:5 that says *"Praise Him upon the loud cymbals: praise Him upon the high sounding cymbals!"* To many people throughout the bitter years of World War I, the hymn became an anchor of hope.

In 1922 several of Prokhanoff's hymn booklets in Russian were published by the American Bible Society in a large volume entitled "Songs of the Christian" in New York City. This book was then translated into Russia and widely used across Eastern Europe. The *modern* English version of this beautiful song was written by Stuart K. Hine. He was born in 1899 in The Grove, a leafy Hammersmith avenue of London. He was duly dedicated to God by his parents at the local Salvation Army. Bought up in a warm Christian home, Stuart dedicated his life to the Lord in 1914 via the ministry of Madame Annie Ryall. His love for the preaching of Charles Spurgeon and of gospel music encouraged him to join Tower Hamlets Choir. Later he was called up for war service in the British armed forces at the age of eighteen. He married in June 1923 and nine years later the couple dedicated themselves to missionary work in Eastern Europe.

During their spell as missionaries in the Ukraine, Stuart came across the Russian translation of the song "How Great Thou Art" in the book of evangelical hymns from the American Bible Society. Immediately impressed by the song, Stuart set about translating the song into English adding to the original with verses of his own. Mr. Hine took additional inspiration for his version of the song from personal experience. The first stanza came about after he experienced an awesome thunderstorm in Czechoslovakia that he told me displayed God's awesome power, the second stanza from walks in quiet mountain forests in Romania. In the third stanza Mr. Hine drew upon his own personal knowledge of the saving Grace of God.

After completing these verses, the Hines returned home to the UK in 1948 and began working with the countless refugees who were fleeing from the Communist persecution in Eastern Europe. Stuart told me, *"What struck me about the mass departure into England in large numbers was the fact that these refugees, in spite of having found greater freedom in their adopted British Isles, continually asked when they would be able to return to their beloved homelands. These requests inspired me to pen the last stanza that talks about the anticipated joy of Christians as they look forward to the second coming of Christ when He will take them to their 'home' to be with Him!"*

"How Great Thou Art" has been adopted as the theme songs of numerous organisations down through the years. Indeed, so many people heard the song that when it was sung at the Billy Graham New York Crusade, people were able to experience the joy of singing this great hymn together with thousands of others! Apparently, the song was sung a total of ninety nine times alone during that Crusade and it became the unofficial theme song of that event.

In 1954 Ulster-man, Dr. Edwin Orr heard the song sung by Naga tribesmen in India and introduced it to audiences in California. In California it was heard by Tim Spencer of the Sons Of The Pioneers cowboy vocal group. He was also the owner-publisher of Manna Music who also wrote the popular "Room Full of Roses" song. Tim heard his son and daughter singing "How Great Thou Art" and was captivated by it. He then secured the American copyright from the author (who retained worldwide rights elsewhere).

The English version of the song has been recorded numerous times and by many famous singers, both Christian and secular, such as Elvis Presley, Pat Boone, George Beverly Shea and the Blackwood Brothers. Stuart K. Hine (he always insisted that the "K" part of his name was used!) went to be with the Lord on 14 March 1989, passing away peacefully in his sleep and the age of ninety two. His memorial service was held at the Gospel Hall, Martello Road, Walton-on-Naze in England at which his version of this tremendous song was sung .

O Lord My God! when I in awesome wonder
Consider all the works Thy hand hath made,
I see the stars, I hear the mighty thunder,
Thy power throughout the universe displayed:

Then sings my soul, my Saviour God to Thee,
How great Thou art! How great Thou art!
Then sings my soul, my Saviour God, to Thee,
How great Thou art! How great Thou art!

How I Love Thee
Keith & Melody Green

'Herein is love, not that we loved God, but that he loved us, and sent his Son to be the propitiation for our sins.'
(1 John 4:10)

If anyone could write an informed book of experience about subjects such as the occult, drugs, therapies, philosophies and the age-long search for the reality it was, Keith Green! Born into a musical family in busy Brooklyn, New York in 1953, he was surrounded by the sound of music. His dear mother sang with the big bands of the day and his grandfather wrote for musical star of the Thirties, Eddie Cantor. A young achiever, Keith began playing the ukelele at three years of age, the piano at six and writing songs by the time he was eight! At age eleven he had become the youngest ever member of ASCAP (the American Society of Composers and Publishers). He appeared in TV commercials and recorded for the major Decca Records label.

His parents were Jewish, yet for some reason, he was brought up as a Christian Scientist. Despite having a natural pride in his Jewish background, he found both religions to be inadequate in his search for reality. *"Throughout the Sixties and Seventies of my youth",* he said, *"I shunned the conventions of the establishment. In the culture of materialism, I become acutely aware of my spiritual need for something deeper in this life!"* Working in hippie songwriters' bars, he spent his search writing songs about how "there must be something more to life than this!" His hate of churches and all things 'happy-clappy' led him to unwisely decide that of all the possible spiritual options, Jesus would be his absolutely last consideration! It was not until all his other philosophical experiments into spiritual fulfilment left him and no other options remained that he kneeled and prayed. *"Oh, Jesus I'm praying to you, asking you if you're real to make yourself known to me!"*....And He did!

"In two years", Keith said, *"I was totally delivered from the occult, drugs and the whole desire to make it in the world! Christ even brought me a beautiful wife, Melody!"* There followed several years of intensive Bible study, discipleship and evangelism. Anyone invited to the Green household was seen as a potential candidate for evangelism!

Throughout the Seventies, Keith Green probably did more to theologically challenge America's gospel music scene than anyone else! With his acute hatred for all things un-Godly, he shunned the Christian music industry as it was, for being wishy-washy and weak, accusing those involved for doing it for personal motives such as gain and fame. He refused to charge for admission to his concerts, giving away his recordings for free! Keith acknowledged that *'Christian music, at best, is a very poor and weak instrument of the gospel. Potentially it can communicate the truth of God; the joy of the Lord; one's Christian experiences; and even warnings of judgement!'* But he also realised that if Christian music did not remain commercially pure, it would cease to do the job God had intended. He was aware that young impressionable Christian kids might unwisely put their favourite Christian singers on a pedestal, replacing their favourite pop idols. *"There is a fine line between idolising the person and real appreciation or admiration!"*

He and his wife Melody chose to give up their home and live in a community of Christians, forming what was to become 'Last Days Ministries', pooling their money and dividing it between the community group or giving it to the needy. Last Days Ministries eventually grew into a full time organisation which ran a Christian training school for young people, producing millions of tracts for distribution and producing a free newsletter-magazine which featured articles from such people as Leonard Ravenhill, Winkie Pratney and David Wilkerson along with those by Keith himself.

During his short lifetime Keith upset the gospel music establishment, exposing faults like pride, fame, greed, arrogance and routine where there should have been God-led humility and grace. Undoubtedly he 'put noses out of joint' with his no-nonsense communications. Wholeheartedly he pursued high motives, above all - the desire to love God and introduce others to the Christ who had revolutionised his life. His active life was cut dramatically short in July 1982 when he tragically perished in a wreckage of a small private plane. Yet even after his death and into the new millennium, Keith's call to discipleship and missionary service still rings out loud and clear in his story and songs! *"How I love You"* speaks of the earnestness of his commitment to His Lord and His purposes.

I was so lost,
But You showed the way,
'Cause You are the Way.
I was so lost,
But You showed the way to me!

How I love You,
You are the One,
You are the One.
How I love You,
You are the One,
God's risen Son.
You are the One for me!

I Am Redeemed
Jessy Dixon

'Forasmuch as ye know that ye were not redeemed with
corruptible things, as silver and gold, from your vain
conversation received by tradition from your fathers;
But with the precious blood of Christ,
as of a lamb without blemish and without spot:
Who verily was foreordained before the foundation of the
world, but was manifest in these last times for you!'
(1 Peter 1:18-20)

Apart from Jessy Dixon, it's difficult to recall another gospel artiste in his musical genre who has survived the decades with such integrity, class and flair. Remaining ever youthful, his rise to world-fame came through the medium of his plentiful hit records on several labels. His multiple appearances on stage and screen in venues ranging from the largest auditoriums to the humblest churches.

With looks and the occasional vocal 'whoop', he vocally reminds one of the legendary Little Richard (*'Rip It Up', 'Tutti Fruiti'* and *'Long Tall Sally'*). But that's where the similarity ceases! Jessy's gospel music heavily influenced the *'rock 'n roll'* generation pointing them to clean cut, wholesome, Christian values. The public has it seems an insatiable desire to hear and sing more of his soul repertoire.

The most requested of Jessy Dixon songs is his happy song, *'I Am Redeemed'* that borrows vivid imagery from the dark days of human slavery. It pictures the scene in the slave market and tells the testimony of a slave who was purchased by a kind benefactor and then set free. In Jessy's mind, inspired by the Apostle Peter's declaration, that is just the spiritual experience that he testifies of through his uplifting gospel music. In the Bible, "to redeem" means "to free someone from some bad fate by paying a penalty, or a ransom". In the ancient Greek world slaves could be redeemed by the payment of a price, either by someone else or by the slave himself. Similarly, Jessy Dixon's song reminds us that Christ Jesus redeems believers from the "curse of the law" and "all wickedness".

Growing up in sunny San Antonio, Texas, Jessy admits that he only initially attended his local church for the enjoyment of its joyous music! His undeveloped faith at that time did not match the God-given gift of his exceptionally good voice. His musical gifting enabled him to graduate as a music major from St. Mary's College. It was while he was at the high school that he came to the notice of renowned gospel artist, James Cleveland.

Moving to Chicago to become a vocalist, accompanist and composer for James Cleveland, singer Jessy's career began to take off under James' auspices. He then formed the Jessy Dixon Singers and attained twelve hit albums. But until this time, his interest was still only in singing soul-styled gospel music, not in the One who he was singing about. Jessy he had not personally surrendered to the claims on his life of Christ Jesus as his Lord and Saviour. This all changed dramatically in 1972 when a close friend told him directly that he needed Christ Jesus in his life. His friend invited him to attend a Bible study group with him where they were discussing the Apostle Paul's book of Romans. After listening to the challenging discussion and then hearing the same message from a radio evangelist, Jessy finally, gave his life to Christ Jesus. There was to be no turning back. Jessy has since gone on to enthusiastically spread the Good News via his singing.

Comfortable and confident before a microphone, he is always powerful in communication. On stage, Jessy's concert tours with Paul Simon (ex-of 'Simon and Garfunkel' fame) helped make him a truly secular international show biz star as well being a gospel music celebrity over several decades.

Through several decades, Jessy's great gospel songs have delighted millions in a career and ministry of outstanding continuing longevity! In recent years, Jessy's singing on the Bill and Gaither Homecoming video series introduced him to a brand new type of audience. His inspiring vocals and presence evoked considerable increased public response thoughout the globe as the videos charted worldwide. *"I'm proud to be a 'bridge-builder!"* Jessy says, *"I detest labels of division such 'Southern Gospel', 'Black Gospel', 'Pop Gospel' or 'Country Gospel' because I can confidently declare that we are all one in Christ Jesus!...I have many examples of many wonderful songs that God has given me down through the years. Sometimes the songs were sung by me solo while others featured my Jessy Dixon Singers and the Chicago Community Choir."*

He says, *"When I was a little boy, I was heard by two people who changed my life. Firstly, there was Mahalia Jackson who (to my embarrassment) told everyone she met that I would follow in her footsteps one day and take the gospel around the world! She was right!...The second person was the late James Cleveland. He said, 'I'm gonna pass the baton to you Jessy, just hold on a little while longer'....to which I wrote a song with that title. 'Hold On A Little While Longer' became one of my first hits!"*

An interesting side factor arising from the huge success of the Gaither Homecoming video series at the turn of this new millennium is the blending together of the black and white musical cultures in ways that have never been seen before. White country performers are comfortably delving into black music repertoire while legendary black artistes like Jessy Dixon are often singing songs penned by the likes Hank Williams, Bill Gaither and Rusty Goodman, songwriters from the bastion of white musical culture. Indeed nowadays, it has been said that *"What Charley Pride is to Country Music, Jessy Dixon is to Country Gospel Music!"* It is only in the Twenty-first Century that Jessy's 'Southern gospel' sound has matured. Nowadays, his southern country roots are showing through with Jessy's great singing sometimes backed by fiddle, steel and mandolin introducing him to new audiences and awakening considerable increased public discovery thoughout the globe.

Jessy's song reminds us that "the ransom price of the redeemed" is not silver or gold. Rather redemption comes via Christ's blood, His death, indeed Christ Himself! The joyous result is the "forgiveness of sins" and "justification". Jessy says, *The Old Testament sacrifices were types (foreshadowings) of Christ depicting His ultimate and only effective sacrifice! Thus Christ the Redeemer was the Passover lamb who took away the sins of the world! God knew before creation that it would be necessary for Christ to redeem man. But He has revealed Christ in these last times!"*

I am redeemed, bought with a price!
Jesus has changed my whole life.
If any body asks you just who I am,
I want you to tell them,
I am redeemed!

Jessy Dixon (Copyright © Dixon Music Company/ EMI Christian Music/ Adm. by CopyCare, PO Box 77, Hailsham, BN27 3EF, England.) music@copycare.com / Used by permission

I'd Rather Have Jesus
Rhea Miller & George Beverly Shea

'*Wherefore also it is contained in the scripture,*
Behold, I lay in Sion a chief corner stone, elect, precious:
 and he that believeth on him shall not be confounded.
Unto you therefore which believe he is precious:
 but unto them which be disobedient, the stone which the
builders disallowed, the same is made the head of the
corner,'
(1 Peter 2:6-7)

Born in Winchester, Ontario, George Beverly Shea's long life spanned the entire Twentieth Century. His was a revered name known worldwide, in the words of steel-guitarist-Bud Tutmarc, as *"a Beloved Christian Singer of the truths of God's Word"*. George Beverly Shea's singing was always a blessing because listeners sensed that his singing came from his heart, not just his vocal chords and mind. His singing of great hymns (like his self penned, *"The Wonder Of It All"*, *"I Will Praise Him"* and the co-penned *"I'd Rather Have Jesus")* blessed millions leaving a lasting impressive legacy.

Life-long partners in evangelistic-song performing, George Beverly Shea (the soloist) and Cliff Barrows (the song leader) are legendary but both are also first-class songwriters. Their touring partnership lasted from World War II into the Third Millennium supporting evangelist-Dr. Billy Graham. Billy always insisted that he wanted George Beverly Shea to sing before he spoke. His reason was simple. He said that no other gospel singer other than the tall Canadian, in his view, moved the audiences to the reverence required to precede his preaching. Billy added, *"I believe music speaks to hearts frequently where sermons fail. Over the years Bev's voice has ministered to people everywhere and will continue to do so until our Lord returns. Someone has said that preaching will be no longer needed in heaven but music and singing will be enjoyed throughout Eternity!"* With a cheeky grin on his face, Billy would add jokingly, *"In heaven I'm gonna be out of a job but Bev will be working harder than ever!"*

Described as the most influential and most popular gospel singer of the last Century, Bev's name and rich baritone voice are known on every continent as a result of his fifty-plus years of association with Dr. Graham. Yet, conversely, he is humble and unassuming in nature. His rise from an inconspicuous administrator in a little New York insurance function to the world's best-known gospel singer is a phenomenal change of career that he would modestly always describe as "a divine call". Career-wise, there was no burning desire for fame or fortune.

Bev says, *"I surrendered to the claims of Christ in my early boyhood years as I carefully observed the simple sincere faith of my dear Christian parents. Their godly prayers for me-their son- played their part too. It's the old, wonderful story confirming once again for those who have faith in the Lord and pray, all things are possible!"* Bev dedicated the entirety of his long life, a living testimony of service, to the Lord he came to more progressively love as decades role by.

Born on the cold first day of February 1909, he was the son of a Methodist preacher Father and a church piano- playing Mother, the fourth of eight brothers and sisters. Bev, as he was affectionately called at home, was the nickname that stuck! Raised in Winchester near Ontario, Canada, his earliest public singing was in his Father's Church. One bright eventful morning in 1933 in his home, his Mother conspicuously left the hand-written poem of Rhea Miller, *'I'd Rather Have Jesus'* on the piano where Bev was due to rehearse. The devotional lyrics (that later caught the attention of the King of

England on a Canadian royal tour) caught Bev's attention that day. *"But what is more important"*, Bev explained to me, *"the sentiment captured my heart. Soon I composed the lilting melody which when married to the lyrics became world-famous."*

Years later, Bev progressed into radio work but turned down many lucrative secular offers knowing that his voice was dedicated to the cause of Christ. Finally, the opportunity came in 1944 to share in a popular hymn programme called "Songs In The Night" featuring an unknown pastor from Western Springs, Illinois, named Billy Graham. So began the lifetime association of fruitful service. Later the duo became a trio of dedicated co-workers as song-leader Cliff Barrows joined them. Cliff recalls with great affection, *"God has given Bev a wonderful gift. My memory overflows with the numerous occasions that his rich and vibrant singing has brought inspiration and strength. It is as though Bev offers a personal plea in song to the Holy Spirit to visit every soul with His saving grace. No wonder, Mr. Graham always wanted Bev to sing before he spoke. Few singers make ready the hearts of an audience like Bev! People were moved to veneration and praise to our Lord when he sang!"*

Bev gave his being to the task of "singing the gospel" and like his preaching and song-leading partners, he successfully contributed to the fulfilment of Christ's Great Commission in the last Century. The crooning movie star Pat Boone stated to me, *"Effective true-blue gospel music like the word of Scripture should be full of grace and truth! That's an apt and wonderful description of the music of George Beverly Shea! It's also an appropriate description of his lifelong humble service. His deep resonant tones have for decades lovingly called people to their individual Hour of Decision. His superb sacred songs have always been high in doctrinal integrity (which is truth!) But I commend my friend Bev Shea most of all for never failing to share the Amazing Grace of God found in our Saviour the Lord Jesus Christ!"*

I'd rather have Jesus than silver or gold,
I'd rather be His than have riches untold;
I'd rather have Jesus than houses or lands,
I'd rather be led by His nail-pierced hand.

Than to be the king of a vast domain
And be held in sin's dread sway;
I'd rather have Jesus than anything
This world affords today.
I'd rather have Jesus than men's applause,
I'd rather be faithful to His dear cause;
I'd rather have Jesus than world-wide fame,
I'd rather be true to His holy name.

In The Garden
C. Austin Miles

'And when she (Mary) had thus said, she turned herself back, and saw Jesus standing, and knew not that it was Jesus. Jesus saith unto her, Woman, why weepest thou? whom seekest thou? She, supposing him to be the gardener, saith unto him, Sir, if thou have borne him hence, tell me where thou hast laid him, and I will take him away. Jesus saith unto her, Mary. She turned herself, and saith unto him, Rabboni; which is to say, Master.
(John 20:14-16)

'In The Garden' was written by the itinerant evangelistic singer, C. Austin Miles in March, 1912 following a request from music publisher Dr. Adam Geibel to write a hymn that would bring hope and comfort to people who were experiencing sickness and anxiety and nearing the end of their earthly life. Years later, the outspoken singing preacher, Hovie Lister of the Statesmen Quartet remembers how he would accompany Austin Miles on the piano. Hovie told me, *'I used to laughingly joke that God never intended for Christianity to sing the blues or wear a long face. The realities of everyday life, however, sometimes dictate somewhat differently as seasons inevitably must change from sunshine to rain. Yes, truly, according to wise old King Solomon, there is a time to laugh and a time to weep! Doubtless, the tragic death of Christ on the Cross devastated the disciples' enthusiasm and joy but only for a season. They slowly came to terms with losing and then re-gaining their well-beloved Messiah. Such a blow as Good Friday was devastating but not crushing! 'In The Garden' by my friend C. Austin Miles speaks of faith reborn in Mary on Easter Day!'*

C. Austin Miles was born in Lakehurst, New Jersey on 7 January 1868. After leaving the Philadelphia College of Pharmacy and the University of Pennsylvania, he worked as a pharmacist for several years.

However, Austin's talents as a songwriter were to lead him into a career of an entirely different nature. After writing his first gospel song, in high hopes he submitted it to the Hall-Mack Publishing Company of Philadelphia. His songwriting potential was recognised accordingly and so eventually he left his pharmaceutical career to work full time for Hall-Mack.

In a well documented interview in 'Forty Gospel Hymn Stories' by George W. Sanville, Austin Miles said:-

'One day in March, 1912, I was seated in the dark room, where I kept my photographic equipment and organ. I drew my Bible toward me; it opened at my favourite chapter, John 20 - whether by chance or inspiration let each reader decide. That meeting of Jesus and Mary had lost none of its power to charm.

As I read it that day, I seemed to be part of the scene. I became a silent witness to that dramatic moment in Mary's life, when she knelt before her Lord, and cried, 'Rabonni!'

My hands were resting on the Bible while I stared at the light blue wall. As the light faded, I seemed to be standing at the entrance of a garden, looking down a gently winding path, shaded by olive branches.

A woman in white, with head bowed, hand clasping her throat, as if to choke back her sobs, walked slowly into the shadow. It was Mary. As she came to the tomb, upon which she placed her hand, she bent over to look in, and hurried away. John, in flowing robe, appeared, looking at the tomb; then came Peter, who entered the tomb, followed slowly by John. As they departed, Mary reappeared;

leaning her head upon her arm at the tomb she wept. Turning herself, she saw Jesus standing, so did I. I knew it was He. She knelt before Him, with arms outstretched and looking into His face cried 'Rabboni!'

I awaked in full light, gripping the Bible, with muscles tense and nerves vibrating. Under the inspiration of this vision I wrote as quickly as the words could be formed the poem exactly as it has since appeared. That same evening I wrote the music.'

C. Austin Miles became an editor with the Rodeheaver-Hall-Mack publishing company and also a popular music director at camp meetings and evangelistic campaigns. He travelled extensively including visits to the American South where he teamed up with Hovie Lister on the piano. Austin died aged 78 in Pitman, New Jersey on 10 March 1946.

On that first great Resurrection Day morning while (as C. Austin Miles' song so poetically says), the dew was still on the roses, Mary experienced how Christ walked and talked with her along the way. It has been said that perhaps Jesus appeared first to Mary because she needed him most at that time. Her crying and wailing were loud expressions of grief. There in the early morning sunshine of the Garden, she did not realise that it was the resurrected Jesus whom she encountered. A number of times the risen Jesus was not recognised because perhaps He may have looked different, or He may intentionally have prevented recognition. Then He spoke her name, *'Mary!'* His voice was familiar and drew forth the loving emotional response from her, *'Rabboni!'*. The word was a strengthened form of Rabbi. Although the word means 'my teacher', there are few if any examples of its use in ancient Judaism as a form of address other than in calling on God in prayer.

I come to the garden alone
While the dew is still on the roses.
And the voice I hear, calling on my ear,
The Son of God discloses.

And He walks with me
And He talks with me

And He tells me I am His own
And the joy we share as we tarry there
None other has ever known.

I Saw A Man
Arthur Smith

*'Jesus answered and said, ...Now is the judgement of this
world: now shall the prince of this world be cast out.
And I, if I be lifted up from the earth, will draw all men
unto me.
This he said, signifying what death he should die.'
(John 12:30-32)*

The beautiful southern city of Charlotte, North Carolina is the home
town for the Arthur Smith Studios, a celebrated venue that has
resounded to many classic recordings. Arthur was initially known
professionally as Arthur *'Guitar Boogie'* Smith after his famous 1947
instrumental hit that was probably country music's first multi-million
selling instrumental. In Europe, it was popularised by the English
guitarist, Bert Weedon. Arthur's sales on "Guitar Boogie" exceeded
three million. The tune heavily influenced the expanding new genre
that became known as rock 'n' roll.

A fact that caused him much ridicule as he grew up, Arthur was
born on April Fools Day (1 April 1921) in Clinton, South Carolina.
Raised in nearby Kershaw, his father, Clayton Smith was a loom
repairer in the textile mill. Horn music of a Dixieland jazz variety
was Arthur's initial musical interest. Then later, he became a famed
multi-instrumentalist (guitar, banjo, fiddle, mandolin) and vocalist
with "RCA Bluebird" in the late Thirties. Ten years later, he finally

shared top billing with "the Hillbilly Shakespeare"-Hank Williams on the prestigious MGM record label. In the early Forties, service with Uncle Sam saw Arthur drafted to the US Navy until the end of World War II.

A committed family man, he settled in Charlotte and his marriage to Dorothy Byars lasted a lifetime. They parented three children-Arthur Reginald, Robert Clayton and Constance Adele.

Country star, George Hamilton IV says, *"Many key country and Christian artistes came under Arthur Smith's skilled studio direction as an album producer. He composed and recorded 'Duelling Banjos' under its original title of 'Feudin' Banjos' on MGM. It was a novel melody that seemed to get one instrument answering another. He successfully proved ownership of the tune in a famous litigation dispute with the makers of the Hollywood movie, 'Deliverance'! Avoiding the magnetic pull of Nashville, he is a successful business person and quality songwriter. Among his best known songs are 'Acres Of Diamonds', 'The Fourth Man' and 'I Saw A Man'."*

An early achiever, Arthur hosted his first radio show at the tender age of fourteen. With TV and radio interests, he also fronted his Crossroads Quartet and Crackerjack Band for many years. A close friend of Billy Graham and his evangelism team, many *country* and *gospel* artistes have utilised the 500 plus Smith song repertoire and studios consistently. Big-time artistes who have recorded Smith's tunes include the Statler Brothers, Pat Boone, the Blackwood Brothers, Johnny Cash, Paul Wheater, George Hamilton IV (who did an entire Arthur Smith album) and George Beverly Shea. Indeed by 1999, Bev Shea recorded no less than twenty-two Arthur Smith songs!

Arthur's song "I Saw A Man" focuses on Jesus Christ as a Man. Arthur says, *"My song is a song about a conversion. Some people (like the Apostle Paul) accept Christ late in life and others at an early age. Conversion comes in different forms to different people. A man can make his world right because Jesus died on the cross to save us from our sins! Perfectly balanced with the Divinity of Christ was the humanity of Christ-the Son Of Man. The expression- the Son Of Man- found in the Old Testament was used as a self-description of Jesus in the New Testament!"*

In Hebrew, "son of man" means an individual man, a man from the genus man. This phrase was used once by the Lord in addressing Daniel and over 80 times in addressing Ezekiel. Probably the Lord wanted to emphasize to them that they were, after all, only men of the earth, in spite of this privilege of receiving the divine word. In Daniel 7:13-14, this phrase is used to describe an individual whom Daniel saw in a night vision, a messianic figure predictive of the Lord Jesus Christ. Jesus called himself "Son of Man" (82 times in the Gospels). He took it from Daniel's prophecy, which must have been familiar to the Jews. Jesus, in assuming this title, was saying to the Jews, *"I am the Son of man in that prophecy!"* Jesus positively used the title in a variety of contexts. For instance, He used it in substitute for "I" when making His important declarations and claims. These concerned His resurrection, His glorious state as the exalted Son of Man, His return to earth in glory, His role in judgment, and most important of all, His passion and violent death.

A man of much skillful humour, Arthur has always used funny anecdotes in his communication. This he combined with being an eager Bible student and Sunday school teacher using his scriptural knowledge to enhance the theological depth of his songs. In 1991, he authored his first book entitled "Apply It To Life" (Thomas Nelson Publishers).

'Then came Jesus forth, wearing the crown of thorns, and the purple robe. And Pilate saith unto them, Behold the man!'
(John 19:5)

It Is No Secret
Stuart Hamblen

*'Jesus answered and said unto them, Go and show John
again those things which ye do hear and see:
The blind receive their sight, and the lame walk, the lepers
are cleansed, and the deaf hear, the dead are raised up,
and the poor have the gospel preached to them.
And blessed is he, whosoever shall not be offended in me.'*
(Matthew 11:4-6)

The cowboy songwriter, Stuart Hamblen recognised that there is
encouraging reassurance in the "Open Secret" of seeing lives changed
by God's power. Once when pressed by a sceptical journalist, he
said, *"To those with eyes to see, it is no secret what God can do!"*
That was also the cheering message that Jesus Christ sent to John
the Baptist by way of John's disciples. Despite John imprisonment,
John's disciples kept in contact with the prisoner and continued his
ministry. In view of the tragedy of John's imprisonment, they asked
Jesus, *"Are you the Messiah or should we expect someone else?"*
For years as a forerunner, John had announced the coming of the
Christ. But now he found himself languishing in prison for months,
and the work of Jesus had not brought the results John apparently
expected, his disappointment was natural. He wanted reassurance
and perhaps also wanted to urge Jesus to further action.

"Report to John what you have seen and heard! It is no secret what God can do!" In this answer, Jesus pointed to His healing works and life-restoring miracles. He did not give promises but clearly observable evidence, evidence that reflected the predicted ministry of the Messiah.

Stuart Hamblen-the wrier of "It Is No Secret" was born on 20 October 1908 in Kellyville, Texas. As he grew, he loved the freedom of the open range and the songs of the cowboys. Show business beckoned and soon he was making a name for himself as a very popular singer on the USA's West Coast. He came to great fame in the Thirties and Forties during the "golden age" of Hollywood's singing cowboys. Movie stars such as Gene Autry, Roy Rogers, John Wayne, Tex Ritter, Rex Allen, Randolph Scott and the like were his close buddies. He rode along side them in their movies usually playing one of the bad guys! Songs such as "Remember Me, I'm The One Who Loves You", "Texas Plains" and "My Mary" penned by Big Stu became established standards. Indeed, Hamblen material was regular repertoire for all the silver screen cowboys, the country stars of Nashville and the great crooners of the time.

Drink and horses were passions that led Big Stu into various moral pitfalls. In 1949 he was convicted in his conscience of his sin and waywardness of life. He initially responded by literally shaking his fist in the face of the young, blond evangelist from the hills of North Carolina. Billy Graham's call to repentance, challenged Big Stu to eventually yield to the claims of Christ. Held in Los Angeles, it was Billy's first major city crusade. James Blackwood of the Blackwood Brothers told me, *'A famed newspaper publisher in Los Angeles was so impressed by the Billy Graham phenomenon that he gave the instruction to all his newspapers to 'puff Graham' nation-wide! That meant provide positive nation-wide publicity!'* The Graham Crusade and the Hamblen conversion hit the national headlines. As far as Stuart was concerned, his friends and foes were bitterly cynical! *"How long would it last?"* was their cynical question.

But last it did! Into old-age the Hamblen lifestyle was radically converted, changed dramatically for the better. In latter years, he penned quality sacred songs such as "Until Then", "Known Only To Him" and "He Bought My Soul At Calvary" (recorded by Stu Phillips,

Bev Shea, Slim Whitman, Jo Stafford, Elvis Presley, Kate Smith and many others). His best known composition was "This Old House" that hit the charts big-time, decades apart via Rosemary Clooney (of Hollywood) and Shakin' Stevens (of Wales). Movie star, John Wayne gave Stuart the idea for "It Is No Secret" while they sauntered together down Hollywood Boulevard. *"Say, Stuart, what's this I hear about you hitting the sawdust trail?"*

"Oh, John my ole Buddy, it's sure no secret what God can do!" With a broad beaming smile, the tall movie actor narrowed his squinting eyes and spoke in all seriousness in his familiar deep tones. *"Stu, you oughta write a song about it!"* That night back home, as the chimes of his grandfather clock struck midnight, Stuart told me that was creatively inspired. Taking pen to paper, words and music of "It Is No Secret" came to him with ease as he sang over to himself.... *"The chimes of time ring out the news another day is through. Someone slipped and fell. Was that someone you?...It is no secret what God can do! What He's done for others He'll do for you!..."*

Since those days, top class acts in great abundance recorded from the Hamblen songbook ranging from Sir Cliff Richard to Mahalia Jackson. It's unusual to note that high-ranking songwriters in their own right, Bill and Gloria Gaither, devoted an entire album to Hamblen material. Seldom if ever does one find song-writing legends of Gaither status saluting another song-writing legend. Cliff Barrows and George Hamilton IV have both separately recorded, on "Word Records", my biographical tribute to Hamblen entitled "The Open Secret".

'I am persuaded that none of these things are hidden...
this thing was not done in a corner.'
(Acts 26:26)

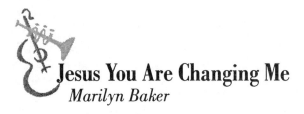

Jesus You Are Changing Me
Marilyn Baker

'And we know that all things work together for good to them that love God, to them who are the called according to his purpose.
For whom he did foreknow, he also did predestinate to be conformed to the image of his Son, that he might be the firstborn among many brethren.'
(Romans 8:28-29)

The theological term used to describe the change that Christ makes in a believer is *regeneration*. It's the work of the Holy Spirit of God and has as its base the idea of 'being born again' or 'being restored'. Though the word regeneration is used only twice in the New Testament, many synonymous passages suggest its basic meaning. Related terms are 'born again', 'born of God', 'quickened' and 'renewed'. Regeneration is the on-going spiritual change wrought in a believer's heart in which the inherently sinful nature is changed and by which he is enabled to respond to God in faith.

The song-"Jesus You Are Changing Me" by Marilyn Baker describes regeneration in her life, an act of God through the immediate agency of the Holy Spirit. His operation in her, originated a new dimension of moral life, a resurrection to new life in Christ. This new life was not merely a neutral state arising out of forgiveness of sin. It was a positive implant of Christ's righteousness by which a believer is made spiritually alive. Marilyn was born of God, made a new creation and given a new life of divine nature!

Marilyn Baker says she was born into a very good home. An only child, her parents ensured that she had everything she wanted materially. Born prematurely and her mother being quite old when she had her, the medical team had to give Marilyn oxygen at birth. Unfortunately, she was given too much and this irrevocably damaged her eyes resulting in blindness. At the age of five she was sent to a boarding school, which was then normal for blind children. Heartbroken, she could only visit her loving parents at weekends in South Birmingham.

At the age of eleven, she went to another school- Chorleywood college in Hertfordshire so she could now only visit her parents once a month. She remembers, *"Whereas I was top of the class at Junior School, I was just one of many at the Secondary School! So I found myself pretty much at the bottom of the class!"*

The oxygen accident also affected her sense of direction. *"All my friends seemed to be able to find their way around school buildings. I was always the slowest making me very unhappy and would often play the fool. I tried doing things to make people like me. But deep down I had a deep sense of insecurity!"*

At the age of fourteen her grandmother died, an event that deeply shocked her as she loved her about as much as she did her mother. The tragedy caused her to start thinking, *"Well, what is life all about then? When death comes is that the end?"* Around the same time, a school Christian Union started up and she was asked her to join. One of the girls in her form said, *"I would like you to meet a couple who take me out on Sundays for tea and things!"* The couple were different from any people Marilyn had met before. As Marilyn recalls, *"They called themselves 'Christians' and I had never met a person who actually said that before! Their family life was different and the atmosphere was different in their house. There were certain things I was not too mad about such as you could not play non-religious records on a Sunday! But there was this love in their lives that really spoke to me. I went along to their church a few times!"*

Later, Marilyn found a book in Braille in the school chapel called "The Transforming Friendship" by Leslie Weatherhead. *"I read it.*

It talked about Jesus in such a personal way mentioning the fact that He is alive and wants to be involved in our everyday lives as a friend. I'd always assumed that He had died 2,000 years ago and maybe He had risen from the dead. But I'd never really understood that He is alive!...Mindful of my wrong behaviour at school, I became fearful that I might have to give account of my actions to God...One night, I just prayed that this Jesus would be my Saviour, that He'd forgive me, and be my friend! Bit by bit my relationship with Him grew and I developed a keenness for the Bible, reading it every minute I could!"

She started attending St. Andrews-the local evangelical Church of England Church and the Brethren Assembly with the friends who took her out on Sundays. It was there she was baptised when she was eighteen. *"These friends proved to be my spiritual parents, helping me with all sorts of questions and doubts!"*

After school, Marilyn attended the Royal College of Music to study oboe and piano. *"I knew I was musical but my harmony teacher said my melodies were boring! I knew that was true. So I just said, 'Lord, if You want me to write I want You to give me a new ability and I want to dedicate my musical talent to you!'...I wrote a song after that, a song of joy called, 'He's My Saviour, My Friend, And My Lord'."*

Marilyn never thought of writing any more. *"I don't know why, I just didn't!' Three years later, I met a friend called Carol who shared her house with me. She didn't have any musical training but possessed a very pleasant voice. So I started to write songs for her. Then I was asked by my minister to share in the evening service. I played the piano while Carol sang!"*

Marilyn continued to write songs and made a custom recording that the singing pastor, Len Magee heard. Realising her gifting should be used, he arranged an interview with London's Pilgrim Records. The result was her first album while she was at Watford Girl's Grammar School teaching oboe. She also taught part-time at Chorleywood College. Loving her job, she did not consider a full-time music ministry at all! In 1982, record company boss, David Payne suggested that she seek God's guidance on her future. After three weeks of praying, she said that God left her in no doubt that

He wanted her to give up her job, which she did! Two days later she received a phone call from a recording company in New Zealand asking her to tour that autumn!

Marilyn Baker's musical ministry touched many people, something that always gladdened her heart. *"We all have our ups and downs in life and I am no exception! So a lot of my songs reflect this! It's wonderful when people come up to me and say, 'We heard your record when we were going through a really down-patch and we found that through it the love of God really came through to us!'"*

Her handicap of being blind caused her some difficulties especially as it resulted in her sometimes not feeling accepted as a natural person. *"I fell it is very important for me and other handicapped people to feel loved for who we are!"* Many times well meaning people would pray for her to be physically healed of blindness. But Marilyn says she accepts God's will in her life saying He accepted her as she was! She says, *"We are all individuals in God's sight! I am thankful that the Lord knows without exception what He's doing with every person!"*

Jesus, You are changing me,
By Your Spirit You're making me like You.
Jesus, You're transforming me,
That Your loveliness may be seen in all I do.
You are the potter and I am the clay,
Help me to be willing to let You have Your way.
Jesus, You are changing me,
As I let You reign supreme within my heart.

Jesus You're The Joy Of Living
Jerry Arhelger & Wes Davis

> *'Now the God of hope fill you with all joy and peace in*
> *believing, that ye may abound in hope, through the power*
> *of the Holy Ghost.'*
> *(Romans 15:13)*

Jerry Arhelger, a man with a funny last name (for the record, it's pronounced Ar-hel-ger) can be found almost anywhere...in a jam-packed college concert of students...in a khaki-uniformed military base concert of soldiers...on the streets of Belfast performing for both sides of the social divide in the open-air...in a football stadium at a major open-air music festival of teens and twenties...in a drab county prison concert of convicts...in a major truck stop concert of rough truckers....or in a sophisticated city concert auditorium. Jerry's talents have taken him to every conceivable gathering place. So powerful was Jerry's testimony and music that he received phone calls from drug addicts and drunks whose lives were put back together again by allowing God to come into their lives.

Jerry Arhelger co-writer of this song was born on 6 April 1951 into a military family which meant that he knew constant movement and uprooting in his early years. His father, Larry who hailed the Lone Star State of Texas was an avid country music fan and this became Jerry's staple musical diet from an early age. *"In my early years,"* Jerry told me, *"I always thought Bob Wills was President,*

Ernest Tubb was Vice President and Hank Williams was Secretary of State!...When I was pickin', I was grinnin!" One of his earliest memories is of hearing Elvis Presley singing in the sunshine of the stadium in Honolulu, Hawaii, from his home 200 yards up the street! It was a style of music that captured his young heart.

Jerry learned guitar and during senior high school formed a competent music group. He was soon on his way to earning a living with a musical career. However, shadows lurked beneath the success. By his mid-teens he was a student of the occult, re-incarnation and mind philosophies. This ended in his taking doctor-prescribed drugs for his nerves, causing him to become heavily dependent on them. But through all the turmoil Jerry had a faithful Christian grandfather praying for his grandson. Consequently in 1971, alone in his car near his home in Wewahitchka, Florida, Jerry had a spiritual experience that changed his life. He surrendered his tortured life to Christ Jesus. Jerry asserts, *"My family and friends thought I'd completely flipped out! But really I'd found that Jesus was the Joy Of Living!"*

A "new person", soon Jerry landed a recording contract on the Herald label, owned by singer and songwriter-Erv Lewis from South Carolina. It was then that Jerry recorded the song, '*Breaker, Breaker, Sweet Jesus'* that was to become a favourite among the truckers and citizen-band radio fans of the time. Success followed and Jerry embarked on a new career as an evangelist and gospel singer. His singing and preaching ministry took him to many countries around the world from major festivals, prisons, conventions, to local churches. George Hamilton IV said, *"Jerry gets my toes tapping. He's a fine person and a real good singer and songwriter with a unique approach. It's kinda country rock, almost a trucking juke box sound we'd expect to hear from the likes of Waylon Jennings. I have been able to observe Jerry close-up and see his story being worked out. He's always got interesting things to say in his music. He often surprises and inspires me!"*

Jerry says that the song-"Jesus You're The Joy Of Living"-is one that he sings in faith not only in times of sunshine but also in times of storm! *"In the Old Testament, joy is commonly a corporately-shared group expression, often associated with dancing or the blessings of prosperity. That's the joy of Christian fellowship! It was accompanied with feasting or offering of sacrifices, in celebration of harvests or victories. The delights of times of prosperity or personal triumphs are all occasions of joy. However, in the New Testament, the word is often found in connection with salvation as well as with eating, drinking and feasting. We all know that life has its changing seasons, its ups and downs, so the New Testament also applies joy to suffering as well as to salvation! Joy comes from life in Christ, drawn from the wells of salvation! It is one of the fruits from the Holy Spirit in each believer!"* In 2001 the song received wide circulation across the USA via the successful 'Praise Street' worship leaders packages put together by Dave Moody, Wesley Pritchard and others.

Jesus, You're the joy of living,
The Saviour of my soul,
The One who made me whole!
Jesus, Jesus, let my whole life shine!
And let the whole world know
That I am Yours and You are mine!

Jerry Arhelger & Wes Davis / New Music Enterprises
© pauldavis@newmusic28.freeserve.co.uk /Used by permission

Let Me Hear You Praise Him
David Moody

'I will sing of the mercies of the LORD for ever:
with my mouth will I make known thy faithfulness to all
generations.'
(Psalm 89:1)

The three Moody Brothers from Charlotte, North Carolina gained international acclaim with what they called their "Americana Music" performing in many distinguished venues such as Wembley Arena (London), the White House (Washington DC) and Disneyland (Paris). The trio's undoubted talents earned them two *Grammy Award* nominations and three International Country Music Association awards. Dave and his brothers started in the early Seventies performing on their parents' local TV show in their home town of Charlotte. Dave himself made his first stage appearance at the tender age of four! His Methodist minister father, Dwight L. Moody Jr, himself a fiddle player, taught all his sons to play musical instruments. *"Music was everywhere in my family"*, Dave recalls, *"it was our life and livelihood!"* At sixteen years of age Dave headed up a folk band in Carolina. Whilst studying *American History* at the *University of North Carolina*, he developed an educational programme aimed at primary school age children. Geared to teaching *American History* using the medium of folk music, it was widely used throughout the State. After college he went on to teach *American History* at

Independence High School in Charlotte for several years. During this time, the Moody Brothers gained a recording contract and went on to *Grammy Award* nominations and a Gold Disc. They were closely involved in the *'Take Pride In America'* campaign from 1987-1992, serving as national spokesmen and performing twice at the White House for two Presidents, Ronald Reagan and George Bush. Dave left the Moody Brothers to concentrate on a solo gospel music career. His first gospel album *'I Will Follow You'*, recorded in Nashville and Charlotte, showcases his many musical talents-vocals, acoustic guitar, electric guitar, dobro, lap slide guitar, mandolin, dulcimer, percussion, bass and keyboard! Such instrumental prowess made Dave a popular session musician on recording sessions being featuring B.J.Thomas, Paul Overstreet, Radney Foster, George Beverly Shea, Charlie Daniels, Johnny Cash, Doc Watson, Thrasher-Shriver, and the Dixie Chicks, among others.

In the summer of 1999, Dave Moody was leading a group of enthusiastic musicians on a mission trip with Rev. Dana Bryan to sunny Northern Spain. Scheduled was a series of "American Festival" outreach events in association with WorldLink Ministries featuring music, basketball expositions, folk crafts, kids' games, and free typical American cuisine-otherwise known as hot dogs and Coke!

"Early on, it was obvious that many Europeans came to our festival each night looking forward to hearing American music. We drew large crowds in every town", David recalled to me recently, *"and then local pastors would preach the Gospel in Spanish to the audiences. Numerous Spaniards made commitments and accepted Christ during our two-week blitz! The trip proved a major influence on the missionary team as well their listeners. Many on the Team chose to go on more mission outreaches at home and aboard.*

I wanted to do a praise song that would offer a little piece of Americana in its presentation. Thus 'Let Me Hear You Praise Him' was born, a very simple call to worship our Lord. It was set to a driving country-rock but also drew on black gospel as the song goes into a free celebration vamp ending with the joyous proclamation-"I've been born again!" Right away, the song became a favourite of the Spaniards and the Americans.

Several months later, I recorded 'Let Me Hear You Praise Him' and placed it on the Internet website as a downloadable music file. Numerous churches around the world e-mailed me to say they were using this song in their worship services and it reached Number One on MP3.com's Christian Chart!"

Back home, Dave was leading worship at the 6000-seater ,Calvary Church in Charlotte when Dr. E. Glenn Wagoner preached on a sermon series entitled "Come On, Shout Hallelujah!" Dave remembered the sermons well. *"Doctor Wagoner emphasised how truly thankful Christians should be that Christ died so that we might be born again! In his preaching, he said, no matter what's happening in our lives, we all have a reason to shout 'Hallelujah!'...I was honoured when Doctor Wagoner asked our praise team to close the service with 'Let Me Hear You Praise Him!'"*

David stated to me, *"I've always enjoyed knowing what I do through music can actually change or influence someone's life forever. But my missionary trips truly altered my perception helping me realise how I can best utilise my talents to bring people into the awareness and hopefully the acceptance of Christ in their life. God has truly blessed my life! At every step of my career, when one door seemed to be closing, we'd trust God to show us the way...and another opportunity would present itself. It is great to be singing and playing for the Lord. I feel God has truly led me to this point in my life - opening and closing doors at every turn."*

Chorus

Let me hear you praise Him
Let me hear you praise His holy name
Let me hear you praise Him
Jesus Christ our King
Let me hear you praise Him
Let me hear you praise His holy name
Let me hear you praise Him
Jesus Christ our King

Verse

Lift your voices and rejoice
Make a joyful noise unto the Lord

Verse

He has reconciled all things
So let us praise Him and sing

Bridge

Come on, shout Hallelujah
Let me hear you say Amen
Everybody shout Hallelujah
Let me hear you say Amen
Come on, shout Hallelujah
Let me hear you Say Amen
Everybody shout Hallelujah
I've been born again!

Love Lifted Me
James Rowe & Howard Smith

*'I waited patiently for the LORD; and he inclined unto me,
and heard my cry.
He brought me up also out of an horrible pit, out of the
miry clay, and set my feet upon a rock, and established my
goings.
And he hath put a new song in my mouth, even praise unto
our God: many shall see it, and fear, and shall trust in the
LORD.'
(Psalm 40:1-3)*

The lyrics writer of 'Love Lifted Me', James Rowe was born in
1865 in the beautiful county of Devonshire in south west England.
He moved to the United States of America in 1890 with his parents
John and Jane Rowe where they set up home in Albany, New York,
becoming a railroad worker and superintendent of the Hudson River
Humane Society in Albany. Later on in life he took up a career in
songwriting and in editing music journals, he worked for various
publishing companies throughout the United States. With poetic
giftings, his other interest was writing serious and humorous verses
for greeting card publishers. A prolific songwriter, he states that he
wrote more than nineteen thousand song texts but perhaps the best
known of these are 'Love Lifted Me' (that was adapted in the
Seventies and became recording successes for Ray Stevens, B. J.
Thomas and Kenny Rogers) and the beautiful 'I Would be Like Jesus'

made popular by George Beverly Shea at the Billy Graham Crusades. James died on 10 November 1933 in Wells, Vermont.

James Rowe was aware that King David's Psalm 40 was a plaintive prayer for help when adversities like waves of the ocean are overwhelming. The basic cause of the psalmist's distress that placed him in a horrible pit of miry clay, is not specified. However, David concedes that it was occasioned by his sin and aggravated by the gloating of his antagonists. His psalm begins with prayer to God for His urgent help and is followed by a testimony of praise for the God's merciful intervention. Praise to the Lord for David's experience of God's help in time of trouble moved him to sing and testify to others of his faith. This became yet another new song that many people could see and as a result would reverence God accordingly with Godly fear.

The music for 'Love Lifted Me' was composed by Howard E. Smith who was born on 16 July 1883. He died on 21 October 1918 but little is known of him other than that he died Norwalk, Connecticut after a lifetime of Christian service as a musician and organist. It was said that Howard's hands were severely crippled by arthritis. Nevertheless, he still managed to play the piano and together with James Rowe, in Saugatuck, Connecticut wrote the lilting melody of this uplifting hymn which tells of the wonderful supernatural ability of God's love to lift sinners from the trauma of mounting seas of sin and despair.

The lyrics of 'Love Lifted Me' by James Rowe are a beautiful metaphor of salvation. Throughout the scripture, God is called the 'Saviour' and portrayed as the God of Salvation who lifts a man or woman from the seas of judgement. In the Old Testament, salvation referred both to everyday, regular types of deliverance such as from foes, ailments and dangers and to major types of deliverance. Specifically, 'Love Lifted Me' is construed to be a definite expression of God's unique and special involvement in human history called the Salvation of Mankind.

The consummate example of the Salvation of Mankind is the Exodus which involved deliverance from the chains of Egypt, safe journey to the Promised Land, and settlement there as a new people in a new relationship with God. This fore-shadowed the hope of the

Messiah who was to deliver His people from their sins. In the New Testament, Christ Jesus is depicted as the Saviour of sinners, the same title reserved for God in the Old Testament is transferred to Jesus. When a human being repents and believes, that person receives salvation. Because of the life, death, and glorification of Christ Jesus, salvation is a contemporary reality. As James Rowe said, *'When "Love Lifted Me", I was rescued from the control of sin and Satan and given freedom to love and serve God!'*

'He sent from above, He took me,
He drew me out of many waters.'
(Psalm 18:16)

Majesty
Jack Hayford

'*I will speak of the glorious honour of thy majesty, and of thy wondrous works.*'
(Psalm 145:5)

Located in Van Nuys, Los Angeles, the *Church on the Way*, pastored by radio and television preacher- Jack Hayford, originally numbered merely a dozen persons when he took-over! It grew eventually to a thousand members under his outstanding Bible teaching and preaching ministries!

Jack's hymnal chorus-"Majesty", inspired by his sight-seeing trips to Denmark and the United Kingdom, is a psalm to the majestic Lord, the Great King! It exalts Him for his mighty acts and benevolent virtues, the glory of His kingly rule. Jack declares, *"It's apt that all believers praise God's mighty acts, which display His greatness and His goodness in creation, providence and redemption. Praise of God's benevolent virtues, should move all creatures to celebrate the glory of His kingdom!"*

Visiting the historic city of Oxford, England, Jack attended a series of seminars by Dr. Edwin Orr on the subject of revival that he called spiritual awakenings. It was 1977, the time of the Silver Anniversary (25th year) of Queen Elizabeth's reign. Celebrations were in full swing! Jack was stirred by the sense of the historic occasion and the awe of the Queen's royalty. It was at Blenheim Palace (birthplace of Winston Churchill, the great wartime leader) where Jack felt motivated to poetically ponder the awesomeness of the royalty of the King of Kings! Heading back to their hotel, Jack plotted the basis of what was to become the illustrious sounding anthem, "Majesty".

In the last Century's fourth quarter, "Majesty" became a modern-day Christian anthem, just as Jack's dear friend-crooner, Pat Boone-surmised it would.

"The lyrics speak of the Kingship of Christ!" Pat speaks highly of its lofty theme. *"The song, 'Majesty' is a wonderful, regal song that declares so powerfully the truth of the sovereignty of Christ's Kingship. It heralds the day when, as the scripture declares, every knee shall bow before Him and acknowledge Him to be truly-His Majesty-King of Kings and Lord of Lords!"*

Most performers are proud and delighted to receive *one* invitation from Her Majesty Queen Elizabeth II. But Pat is understandably even prouder! Overjoyed, he has received two invitations to Royal Command Performances! Comically, in Pat's case the summons were a cause of more than a little embarrassment on his part! Standing in the tense line-up, sandwiched between eminent movie actors Claudia Cardinale and Peter Finch, Pat was trying to seem very calm and blasé. After all, this was his second Royal Command Performance in London. He even resorted to jabbing fun at those whose nerves were beginning to show visibly, with words of bravado. *"Come on now!...The Queen is just a human being, a woman with an important job, of course, but just a flesh and blood human being like you and me! Why are you so nervous?"*

But pride, as they say, comes before a fall and Pat certainly found it true that evening! The Queen entered the room and he mentally rehearsed what he would say to her, should she stop and talk to him. He reminded himself of the strict protocol that exists on such occasions. She stopped momentarily to speak to Peter Finch and then Pat's nerves fluttered as he realised that she was standing in front of him. Bowing slightly, he articulated the appropriate response. *"Your Royal Highness!"* The Queen greeted him with a regal smile. *"We've met before, Mr. Boone!"* Completely thrown by her comment, he said the first thing that came into his head as he stammered. *"We did...eh...your Majesty?"*

"Yes!" The Queen replied, a twitch of a smile beginning to form on her unruffled face. *"Yes, you came over for another Command Performance and, if I remember correctly, interrupted your studies at school to do it!"* Poor Pat's mind went embarrassingly blank and he could think of nothing to intelligently say in reply but a sentence come from his lips involuntarily. *"I'm glad you're here!"*

Pat cringes and squirms nowadays as he recalls what a dumb thing he said to the Queen of England! The next day, his discomfiture was complete when his picture appeared on the front pages of London newspapers. With the Queen standing before him, Mr. Boone stood there, mouth hanging open and a completely dumbstruck look on his face!

Pat's royal command performances taught him an important spiritual lesson he didn't realise until his Holy Spirit baptism. He noted, *"People everywhere are still awed by royalty. Nobody stirs excitement or demands respect on every level of life like a king or a queen!"* Elated, of course, at every opportunity to sing, Pat's doubly appreciative when he obtains an invitation from a palace. As he declares, he's still awed by royalty! *"I've sung for kings, queens and presidents, several times. I can tell you that it's an exhilarating and frightening experience! It's no use, no matter how many times you tell yourself, 'They're just people, like I am!'-and they are-when you're suddenly confronted with a view of royalty, even from a great distance, your heart pounds. All normal behaviour is suspended and one presses forward with others to see more clearly. One wants to breathe the air around them, to wonder at a life so vastly different from one's own, and perhaps, to catch a fleeting glimpse, even a smile...from a king...a queen...or a president! King David, great as he was, recognised the importance of honouring the King of Kings!"* He said, *'Enter into His gates with thanksgiving, and into His courts with praise: be thankful unto Him, and bless His name. For the LORD is good; His mercy is everlasting; and His truth endureth to all generations!'*

To the only wise God our Saviour,
be glory and majesty, dominion and power,
both now and ever. Amen.
(Jude 25)

May God's Blessing Surround You Each Day
Cliff Barrows

> 'The LORD bless thee, and keep thee:
> The LORD make his face shine upon thee, and be gracious
> unto thee:
> The LORD lift up his countenance upon thee, and give thee
> peace.'
> (Numbers 6:24-26)

A masterful songleader, genial host and impactive speaker, the multi-talented Cliff Barrows was also a quality songwriter as *"May God's Blessing Surround You Each Day"* demonstrates. Dedicating his life in his youth to the service of God, he remained in the saddle to the end of the road! Along with his buddy, Bev Shea, he remained true to the divine call and his team-pact with Billy Graham from the close of World War II to the opening of the new millennium. Cliff will be lovingly best remembered for his choir leading and his powerfully effective, narrative skills with scripture and poetry. One of Cliff's well known poems "The Touch Of The Master's Hand" as also popularised by cowboy movie star, Tex Ritter.

Cliff excelled too with great sing-a-long songs and hymns. George Hamilton IV says, *"How can anyone forget the wonderful, majestic melodies of praise that have characterised the impactive Billy Graham missions of the second half of the Twentieth Century led by Cliff Barrows? I don't believe the Twentieth Century ever saw a more powerful songleader than Cliff! He undoubtedly left his mark on the sands of time with his skills in gospel music, and his dedication to the task of world-wide evangelism. Never one to crave the limelight he would often repeat his choir song, in the words of the blind Victorian poet, Fanny Crosby- 'To God be the glory, great things He has done!'"*

Cliff's lifelong confidant, Billy Graham recalled his first surprising encounter with Cliff in 1945. Cliff was urged to conduct the singing for a youth night service at which Billy was to speak. But Billy recalled with a smile, *"I must in all honesty say, I accepted him dubiously! But my doubts were instantly dispersed by his skill and sunny disposition! Aided by a fine voice, a trombone and the piano-playing of his beautiful wife, Billie, soon he had the audience singing to their fullest capability!"*

So began a historic association as songleader-Cliff, preacher-Billy, and gospel singer-George Beverly Shea hit the road as an evangelistic trio. Their heart-felt quest endured more than half a century taking them worldwide. Only eternity will reveal the full extent of the fruits! Many thousands bore grateful testimony to the life-changing message the trio shared, including myself!

Cliff had a happy- go-lucky exterior that belied his deep sensitivity and discernment. With his ever youthful looks, he was more than just a genial host and songleader. For the giant, globe- trotting, Billy Graham Missions he was actually the "man in charge" until the evangelist himself stepped forward to deliver his message. Able to command authority among his peers, he was fully furnished for the demanding responsibility he displayed.

Born on 6 April 1923 in the little town of Ceres, California (named after "Ceres" the pagan goddess of the harvest), his family had a rural background. His father, a humble farmer, loved the soil and his work in the fields. Those boyhood days in the country held affectionate memories for Cliff as he remembered how he toiled alongside his father *"It was a precious time"*, he recalled to me, *"although I didn't think so at the time!...As I reflect back in later life, I respect my Dad's work ethic, his love of creation, and his work in the fields of harvest. His love has been a great challenge and inspiration to me!"*

The drama of conversion came at the age of eleven as Cliff responded to the claims of Christ and full-time Christian service beckoned. He met the aspiring young preacher-Billy Graham at the close of World War II in the town of Asheville in the hills of North Carolina. Teaming up, a new chapter in Church history was to be written from that time. Single-mindedly and skilfully, Cliff devoted his creativity, time and effort into communicating "the Good News" via a wide variety of media, varying from radio, television and movies to recordings and concerts. Always an enthusiast all his life-long ministry, he stated , *"Every great moving of the Spirit of God has been accompanied by great singing and I believe it always will be!"*

As a life-time co-worker, Billy Graham summed his partner up well when he said, *"Cliff's dedication and sincerity are immediately evident! He gives Christ the chance to live out his life in Cliff, and the results in terms of Christian witness are wonderful to see!"* That other life-time, co-worker with Cliff, his buddy Bev Shea says, *"Cliff's Christ-centred dedication to his song-leading and choir-directing ministry has given him a much deserved, world-wide reputation!"*

Inducted into the "Gospel Music Association Hall of Fame" in 1988 and into the "Religious Broadcasting Hall of Fame" in 1996, he is a man of many skills. But on every continent, it's as a songleader that he'll be remembered! His winning smile and enthusiastic charm motivated thousands to lift their voices in praise of God in song. The majestic musical sounds of the massive Billy Graham Crusades under the direction of songleader Cliff were in their day great musical blessings.

Cliff says his song, *'May God's Blessing Surround You Each Day'* is a musical benediction, a reminder of the Aaronic benediction found in Numbers 6:24-26. *"The prayer asks the Lord to make His face shine upon believers in acceptance, favour and peace! The Hebrew word for peace is shalom! Here its seen in its most expressive fullness-not merely the absence of war, but a positive state of rightness and well-being! Such peace comes only from the Lord!"*

May God's blessing surround you each day
As you trust Him and walk in His Way
May His presence within guard and keep you from sin,
Go in peace, go in joy, go in love!

(Cliff Barrows Copyright © /Used with permission)

Meekness And Majesty
Graham Kendrick

'Tell ye the daughter of Sion, Behold, thy King cometh unto thee, meek, and sitting upon an ass, and a colt the foal of an ass.
And the disciples went, and did as Jesus commanded them, And brought the ass, and the colt, and put on them their clothes, and they set him thereon.
And a very great multitude spread their garments in the way; others cut down branches from the trees, and strewed them in the way.
And the multitudes that went before, and that followed, cried, saying, Hosanna to the son of David: Blessed is he that cometh in the name of the Lord; Hosanna in the highest.
And when he was come into Jerusalem, all the city was moved, saying, Who is this?
And the multitude said, This is Jesus the prophet of Nazareth of Galilee.'
(Matthew 21:5-11)

The scene of Graham Kendick's song "Meekness and Majesty" was old Jerusalem 2000 years ago, the drama was the perfect fusion of meekness and majesty! Prior to His Last Supper with His Disciples, was His Triumphal Entry into the Old City, as prophesied. Jesus

Christ mounted a humble donkey, an animal symbolic of humility, peace and Davidic royalty. He sat on the cloaks and we know from Mark and Luke that He rode the colt. Typically, a mother donkey followed her offspring closely. Matthew mentions both the two animals. The spreading of the people's cloaks on the road was an act of royal homage as was the waving of the branches. The shouts of "Hosanna!" expressed both prayer and praise to the royal Son of David while the expression "in the highest!" was a call to those in heaven also to sing "Hosanna"!

There is no denying that Graham Kendrick has a way with words. His many modern hymns ably demonstrated that his song lyrics theologically took a stand above the rest. Graham admits to starting with an advantage. Raised in Putney Baptist church in south London, he was well apprenticed by his Father, the Minister. Soaked in Bible knowledge from an early age, Graham said it enables him to re-tell many of the familiar scriptural incidents through the eyes of the people there. *"I do so, calling on all the tools that I as a poet have at my disposal - imagery, symbolism and so on. The thing which inspires me is stepping into the shoes of these people. However, I must point out that the source of my inspiration is the living Jesus Christ. As I get to know Him better I hope my songs will picture Him more clearly, not as a picture recalled from the past, but as He is. He is on the throne living in resplendent glory in and among those who belong to His Kingdom on Earth!"*

In the latter Seventies Graham Kendrick became more and more active in partnership with the head of British Youth for Christ, Clive Calver, who went on to head up the English Evangelical Alliance. At the height of his songwriting abilities Graham said that he felt the urgency to not only preach the gospel but to encourage other Christians particularly the young to do likewise. *"Many of us feel"*, he said, *"that we are in the last few years of grace. That's why many of my recordings major on the end times and our Christian responsibilities to a lost and dying World. Before we know it the day will have ended and the night will have come!"*

Graham Kendrick as a musician and composer is a name that epitomises the best of the British contemporary Christian music scene. He achieved the adulation and approval of old and young with his theological musical applications. Yet he chose to quietly slip out of what he said was the lonely world of Christian showbiz where the prevalent disease is caused by spiritual starvation. He sought more meaningful involvement in the Body of Christ and widened his ministry accordingly preferring as he says "to minister rather than perform". "In the mid- Seventies he became burdened about young Christians who wanted to use their musical ability for God's glory but were becoming lost along the way due to lack of fellowship, teaching and belonging. He helped organise retreats for musicians who were serious about their calling. Many musicians testified during those that Graham's ministry heavily influenced their lives and prompted their involvement in organisations like the British Youth For Christ. Later he became associated with Roger Forster who headed up an enterprising group of churches in the south London area known as Ichthus Fellowships. Graham also gave his substantial support to the worldwide phenomenon known as the March For Jesus. Across the world, hundreds of thousands of Christians in city streets demonstrated their faith by taking part in the International March For Jesus.

It was a demonstration that delighted Graham who declared, *"Today the sounds of praise are filling streets all over the World; overflowing from the hearts of people of many nations. And there is one name on all our lips, the name of Jesus Christ! As Christians unite across the continents and islands to march together, the world will have to ask why we are marching and where we are going. We will tell them we are marching for Jesus, we are marching with Jesus, and we are marching to Jesus.*

As the world of 'not yet' believers looks on, they see the radiance on our faces, the reflected glory of the One on whom we are all gazing. They hear our joyful praises in the songs we are singing. They are touched by His love and long for His embrace. As our procession of worship moves majestically towards the throne, we call others to come with us, longing to present them as an offering to the Lamb, that He might receive the rich and full reward of His suffering."

Meekness and Majesty,
Manhood and Deity,
In perfect harmony,
The Man who is God.
Lord of eternity
Dwells in humanity,
Kneels in humility
And washes our feet.

O what a mystery,
Meekness and majesty.
Bow down and worship
For this is your God,
This is your God.

Millennium Prayer
Paul Field & Stephen Deal

'*After this manner therefore pray ye:*
Our Father which art in heaven, Hallowed be thy name.
Thy kingdom come. Thy will be done in earth, as it is in
heaven.
Give us this day our daily bread.
And forgive us our debts, as we forgive our debtors.
And lead us not into temptation, but deliver us from evil:
For thine is the kingdom, and the power, and the glory, for
ever. Amen.'
(Matthew 6:9-13)

"The Millennium Prayer" was a clever musical-marriage adapting
of *"The Lord's Prayer"* to *"Auld Lang Syne"*. The co-writers/
composers, Paul Field and Stephen Deal wrote it for a Rob Frost
musical. Born in South London in1954 and raised in a Christian
home, Paul Field attended the local Baptist Church where his Father
played the organ and his Mother led the Sunday School. At the age
of thirteen years came his nervous introduction to performing before
an adult audience. It initially came when he played music at his
church in a trio formed with the minister's daughter and another
girl-friend. Although he was composing his own songs by this time,
they were not rooted in his own personal experience. *"I didn't have*
a very real understanding of what I was doing or what a Christian
was!" Paul admits, *"The songs I was writing probably had the right*

lyrics but that was purely because of my upbringing. Most of my social life was in the church it was easy to pick up the right phraseology and words. " It was not until he attended a church house-party at the age of seventeen that he says that he committed his life fully to Christ. His first music group (with Pam May and Heather Barlow) was called *Jesus Revolution*, a musical reflection of the Jesus Movement of that era. Their first album was released in 1973 although the group still retained their day jobs as teachers. It was not until 1976 they decided to go into music full time with a name-change. The group, that became known as *Nutshell,* began to tour extensively all over England and Europe, followed by appearances on ITV's *Pop Gospel* programme with two replacement singers Mo McCafferty and Annie McCraig. The group toured extensively with superstar, Sir Cliff Richard during 1979-80 and changed their name to *Network 3.* Despite success, it was not long after that the strains of being on the road started to impinge on plans. Then came the dawning realisation in the trio that things needed to change. *"The trio came to an end purely and simply, "* says Paul, *"because it was meant to! There was a sense of disappointment, but it felt a sense of release for me. I think it's very hard for Christians involved in the arts to maintain a steady walk with God. It should be the core of a Christian's very existence!"*

Paul has since concentrated on being known more for his songwriting and producing abilities rather than as a performer in his own right. *"Writing is far more important to me, "* says Paul, *"and performing before smaller more intimate audiences causes one to be honest because you are not hiding behind the performance. The reason I still play concerts is that I want to share the gift of song that God has given to me. If there are things that people in the audience can find useful or beneficial in the songs then they can take them and use them in their own walk with God!"*

The Lord's Prayer should properly be called *the Disciples' Prayer* since it was not prayed by Christ but rather taught to the disciples by Him. In Luke's Gospel, at the request of a disciple, He gave a modified form of His earlier spontaneous presentation in the Sermon on the Mount. The earlier form is fuller and is commonly used. As a pattern prayer, it is unsurpassed for conciseness and fullness, showing the proper approach and order in prayer. The prayer points forward to the heavenly millennium in its plea that *"thy kingdom come, thy will be done on earth as it is in heaven"!* It was a stoke of genius from Paul that married *'The Lord's Prayer'* to the *'Auld Lang Syne"* tune. The opportune suggestion that Cliff Richard should record it for the 1999 end of year Millennium celebrations was rewarded by seeing the song topping the charts at the consummate time. It captured the public mood and expression with a perfect sense of history!

Inspired in the First Century, the Apostle John foretold about the forthcoming heavenly millennium. *I saw the souls of them that were beheaded for the witness of Jesus, and for the word of God...and they lived and reigned with Christ a thousand years. But the rest of the dead lived not again until the thousand years were finished. This is the first resurrection. Blessed and holy is he that hath part in the first resurrection: on such the second death hath no power, but they shall be priests of God and of Christ, and shall reign with him a thousand years."* This future heavenly millennium of Revelation 20:4-6 (from the Latin *mille,* "thousand" and *annus,* "year") is taken literally by many believers as 1,000 actual years, while others interpret it metaphorically as a long but undetermined period of time. The present form of God's kingdom is moving toward a grand climax when Christ will return, the first resurrection will occur and His kingdom will find expression in a literal, visible reign of peace and righteousness on the earth in space-time history. After the final resurrection, the last judgment and the renewal of the heavens and the earth, this future, temporal kingdom will merge into the eternal kingdom, and the Lord will reign forever on the new earth.

Our Father who art in heaven,
Hallowed by Thy Name.
Thy kingdom come,
Thy will be done on earth as in heav'n
Give us today our daily bread
And forgive our sins
As we forgive each one of those
Who sins against us:

And lead us not to the time of trial
But deliver us from evil
For Thine is the kingdom,
The power and the glory
Let all the people say 'amen'
In every tribe and tongue;
Let every heart's desire be joined
To see the kingdom come.
Let every hope and every dream
Be born in love again:
Let all the world sing with one voice,
Let the people say 'amen'.

One Day At A Time
Marijohn Wilkin & Kris Kristofferson

> *'Take therefore no thought for the morrow:*
> *for the morrow shall take thought for the things of itself.*
> *Sufficient unto the day is the evil thereof.'*
> *(Matthew 6:34)*

No one is immune to those terrible nights spent in bed staring at the ceiling trying to sleep only to be kept awake by the worries of what the following day will bring. It affects all of us irrespective of age or status at some time or other. Worries change with our circumstances.... For a school child, the worries are about bullies or science homework. For an adult, it is about the next morning's presentation in front of the company director. For the mother, it is whether her child's temperature is anything to be concerned about. As we enter our latter years, it is the fear of being left grieving and alone.

Surely one of the most stressful instances any of us find ourselves in is to be in hospital. A few years ago a hospital radio poll was asked to compile its top ten most requested songs, the winner was surprising. The most solicited song came from the pen of a prolific writer from Kemp, Texas, Marijohn Wilkin. Her popular song "One Day At A Time" has a lilting chorus that is really a prayer!... *"One day at a time, Sweet Jesus, that's all I'm asking from You! Lord give me the strength to do everything that I've gotta do!"*... The song pleads to the Lord for the strength to get through each passing day.

Perhaps after all, it's not such a surprise that such a moving song is chosen by people struggling in hospital.

Marijohn was a war widow at the age of just 21. Her young husband, an Allied pilot was shot down in North Africa. As a prisoner of war along with other Allied prisoners, he perished in an enemy submarine escorting them back to Europe. The vessel was attacked by Allied war planes not realising that it carried prisoners of war. Naturally, the news devastated the young wife.

Marijohn now widowed began her working life as a school teacher. As the years rolled by she discovered her love of song writing and changed career path to take on her hobby full time in one of Nashville's writing houses. Whilst there she wrote over 300 songs for a range of artists (ranging from Joan Baez to Stonewall Jackson to Burl Ives to George Hamilton IV). Her song-"PT 109" about John F. Kennedy's wartime naval exploits was featured in a Hollywood movie of the same name. Eventually, she left to set up as a publisher in her own right. The administrative pressures took time and joy away from Marijohn's writing. Steadfastly, she balanced this by creating her own band "The Marijohn Singers" who performed across the USA, recorded for CBS and secured a three year stint on the "Grand Ole Opry" TV Show.

Raised in a highly spiritual home, Marijohn felt that her coming to personal faith was an evolutionary process. As she put it to me, *"There was nothing over emotionally…It was just a way of life!…It was to me just like breathing!"* But as the war clouds thundered across the Forties sky, Marijohn began to loose her spiritual roots. As a young war widow, she said she began to hide her feelings and became "pseudo-sophisticated" and brittle. She claims it was her way of keeping herself from being hurt. In addition, she almost had an overwhelming compulsion to be a "giver" to everyone. She began giving away her time, money and hospitality in a desperate attempt to avoid the pain of her war-torn life. But eventually the strain was too much and she collapsed in tears wondering "Where was the person to help me?"

"One night, I came to the total end of myself," she says, *"…for the first time in my life, I knelt down and cried and cried and cried!…I*

could see that night the solid wall before me and could visualise it finally breaking loose! This was like my own freedom breaking through! Until then, I was a prisoner behind the wall of my own self protection!"

This emotional breakthrough was the beginning of Marijohn's reconciliation to God although it took a few more years of searching and spiritual exploration first. It was not to mature until she suffered the death of a business partner and then her mother, three months later. Then Marijohn found herself caring for her next of kin. Her 88 year old Uncle was dying from a terminal medical condition. For the first time in twelve years, Marijohn left Nashville for Texas for six weeks to care for him. It was his uncomplaining Christian witness in his dying days that so impressed her that she rededicated her life to God.

Her song "One Day At A Time" was co-written by the young movie actor and singer/songwriter, Kris Kristofferson returning from Germany as a helicopter pilot working for Uncle Sam. Kris had been directed to Marijohn by one of her distant relatives impressed by his songwriting.

The lyrics of "One Day At A Time" reflect the honesty that Marijohn has with the Lord in her Christian life. Indeed, it was this honesty that caused it to be recorded in the first instance! *"Kris Kristofferson happened to be recording in Nashville,"* Marijohn remembers, *"and I was anxious to let him hear some of my new gospel songs. Kris came to Johnny Cash's studio and listened while I re-mixed my album. One of the songs on the album was 'One Day At A Time' which I had started and Kris helped me to finish. As Kris heard it played back, he turned his head away and I could tell he was crying. After it was all over he looked at me and said, 'I wanna tell you, Marijohn, that I was afraid that you had contrived a bunch of Gospel songs! But after hearing it I got to admit that it's so totally honest!' Later he went home to California and sent the liner notes to me and when I read them I cried!"*

Kris' notes said, *"Marijohn, sometimes it seems like you've got to go an awful long ways to get back where you started! (Of course, some us do get loster than others!) You and I have probably shared more grief and glory in past years than we thought we deserved - and, no doubt, we'll continue to do so. ...You put me in mind of a line from Blake:*

> *Excess of Sorrow laughs!*
> *Excess of Joy weeps!*
> *Thanks for the feelings! Enjoy the journey!"*...Kris Kristofferson

I'm only human, I'm just a woman.
Help me believe in what I could be and all that I am.
Show me the stairway I have to climb,
Lord for my sake teach me to take one day at a time.
One day at a time, sweet Jesus,
That's all I'm asking from you.
Just give me the strength to do everyday what I have to do.
Yesterday's gone, sweet Jesus,
And tomorrow may never be mine.
Lord help me today, show me the way,
One day at a time.

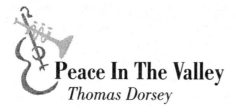

Peace In The Valley
Thomas Dorsey

'The wolf also shall dwell with the lamb,
and the leopard shall lie down with the kid;
and the calf and the young lion and the fatling together;
and a little child shall lead them.
And the cow and the bear shall feed;
their young ones shall lie down together:
and the lion shall eat straw like the ox.
And the sucking child shall play on the hole of the asp,
and the weaned child shall put his hand on the cockatrice'
den.
They shall not hurt nor destroy in all my holy mountain:
for the earth shall be full of the knowledge of the LORD, as
the waters cover the sea.'
(Isaiah 11:6-9)

"Peace In The Valley" penned by the renowned Chicago pastor, Thomas Dorsey (Georgia Tom) has gained a classic reputation. Originally published by Ben Speer of the Speer Family, in error he thought that it was a folk song in "the public domain". Years later, Ben innocently gave it to the Blackwood Brothers Quartet in the mid Fifties to record and it since became a classic. The Blackwoods' version was beloved by an impressionable, truck-driving teenager from Tupelo, Elvis Presley. Years later as a superstar, Elvis recorded the song himself using the Blackwoods' arrangement. Since then, the limelight that Elvis' version gave the modern spiritual, projected it so widely, it has become world-famous, traversing the globe!

Thomas Dorsey was born on 1 July 1899 in Villa Rica, Georgia. He was raised in the poverty of a rural Southland that resented and begrudged the freedom from slavery granted to his parents following the American Civil War. When he left his severely deprived boyhood home, he rubbed musical shoulders with some of the legendary blues and jazz artistes of his day such as Bessie Smith, Ethel Waters and Ma Rainey. Morally, he struggled between such unwholesome influences of drink, gambling and sex, and the benevolent pull of the Holy Spirit! Finally he surrendered to Heaven's claim on his wayward life.

Years later, as the pastor of the Pilgrim Baptist Church in Chicago, he penned some three hundred songs including "Take My Hand Precious Lord" from his heart-rending, personal experience of tragedy. In 1932, booked to go to a St. Louis church revival meeting, upon his arrival after his exhausting journey, he was given devastating news about his wife. Earlier, Nettie bearing their first child, had persuaded him to attend the revival. While still on the revival meeting platform, he was slowly and sensitively told of the death of his dear spouse in painful childbirth by his St. Louis friends (who had heard the news via a telegram). Heartbroken, he immediately rushed to a telephone to confirm the sad news. His friend, Gus Evans offered to accompany him on the painful journey home. Together they drove north, homewards arriving back only to receive yet another blow. Initially, the new-born baby seemed to be doing well but then surprisingly, he too died during the night. Thomas said, *"Funeral arrangements were hastily arranged and both mother and child were interred in the same coffin. I was very despondent for several days as I mourned. I was severely tempted by satan to go back to the world's music. But the Lord held me up and strengthened me!"*

Greatly distressed, initially Thomas drove aimlessly around the streets of the big city. Then as he drove, he conceived under divine inspiration the basics of what was to become the now renowned prayer-in-song, "Take My Hand Precious Lord". Stopping at Madame Malone's College, he visited his friend, Professor Frye. Together they strolled though the peaceful greenery of the college campus. Finally they entered one of the empty music rooms where Thomas parked himself beside the piano. As his lands gently caressed the ivories, a simple melody took shape as Thomas vocalised, *"Blessed Lord! Blessed Lord! Blessed Lord!"*

"Why don't you turn it into 'Precious Lord', Thomas?" Professor Frye enquired. There and then, *"Take My Hand Precious Lord"* crystallised. Later translated into about 35 foreign languages, the composition is accepted today as standard fare with plentiful recordings available.

Years later, contemplating his heavenly home and reunion with missing loved ones, Thomas read the prophet Isaiah's vision of "Peace In The Valley". It was the creative inspiration he needed for Thomas's great inspirational song. The new song spoke of the peace and safety of the Messianic Age reflected in the fact that little children will be unharmed as they play with formerly ferocious animals. Thomas saw such placid conditions and his family reunion as a wonderful description of the future consummation of the Messianic kingdom. Thomas stated, *"Some of my Christian brothers believe that the peace described in this passage has been inaugurated through the first coming of Christ and the preaching of the gospel, and will be consummated at the return of Christ! Some other brothers maintain that it's a prophecy of conditions during a future 1000 years reign of Christ on the earth that follows the last days of history. But I believe that the term the 'last days' can refer to the future generally, but usually it seems to have in view the Messianic Age!"* Thomas knew that in a very real sense, the last days began with the first coming of Christ and will be fulfilled at His second coming.

'Be perfect, be of good comfort, be of one mind, live in peace; and the God of love and peace shall be with you.'
(2 Corinthians 13:11)

Seek Ye First
Karen Lafferty

'But seek ye first the kingdom of God,
and his righteousness;
and all these things shall be added unto you.'
(Matthew 6:33)

The writer of "Seek Ye First"-Karen Lafferty says, *"The Bible teaches that seekers must have faith! They should always remember God's mercies and, above all, count the cost! The act of 'seeking God' was commanded in scripture for salvation. Not that God is difficult to find. Scripture promised that God would be found for pardon, salvation, providential care and spiritual blessings when sought by the seeker with his whole heart!"* Seeking God means seeking His name, His Word, His strength, His commandments, His precepts, His kingdom and, as Karen Laffety's song declares, *"His righteousness"*. The action should be immediate, with the heart, and continuous while He may be found! In return God promises His favour and His protection. Karen stated, *"When the saints seek especially with purpose in their hearts, the end will be praise and rewards!"*

Karen Lafferty was born and raised in Alamogordo, New Mexico and became a born-again Christian at the tender age of ten years. But she readily admits that she lacked the reality of *"a close relationship with Him"*. In college Karen began singing as a soloist and as a member of a rock group. Finishing college, after obtaining a Bachelor of Arts in Music Education at Eastern New Mexico University, Karen pursued a music career performing in seedy New Orleans saloons. Although she admits that her talents were God-given, she says, *"My use of my gift was selfishly just for myself and not for others!"*

The year 1971 became a turning point in her life when she was challenged to think more deeply about what being a Christian really was! Up until then she says that she did not understand the power of the Holy Spirit or the importance of studying and becoming familiar with God's Word, the Bible. With maturity, Karen responded by renewing her commitment to God and attempted to use her talents in Christian music rather than pursuing a secular career.

Shortly after, Karen auditioned for Campus Crusade's music ministry and was duly humbled when her services were politely declined. "My singing was okay", she remembers, "but Campus Crusade wisely saw that I was too young a Christian to be able to handle the responsibilities!"

So even more firmly convinced that the Lord wanted her to continue in show business, she moved to California and began an earnest push for professional notice, as she recalls. *"Between sets in dingy bars and night clubs, I shared my faith in Christ Jesus with the patrons, a practice that didn't go down to well with my employers! But California was where I believed the Lord wanted me to be! I heard a lot of strange things about California but what I didn't know was that God had been really pouring out His Spirit in that area and I prayed I would find a church that was really teaching the Bible; a good solid church where I could grow spiritually. I knew that what I needed was to grow in God's Word!"*

Eventually, her cousins introduced her to Calvary Chapel of Costa Mesa, then in the early stages of its tremendous *Jesus People* growth. There she was delighted to see contemporary music being used to convey the gospel message to other young people and almost immediately she became a part of it. She thus began her Christian music ministry in earnest. Music groups (such as Love Song and Children of the Day) and soloists (Debby Kerner of 'Kids Praise' albums fame) had recorded an album called "Everlasting Jesus Music

Concert". This music ministry eventually was to evolve into the 'Maranatha Music' record label. Karen became actively involved, was part of the second album, playing oboe and guitar.

Before long, Karen was able to give up her night club work and devote all her talents to writing songs about her Lord and performing them for Christian gatherings. *"I believe God called me to the music ministry to minister His love through music. I got involved in evangelism but also felt called to minister encouragement to the body of Christ in churches also! I became involved with Youth With A Mission going out into the highways and byways with the Gospel!"*

Her classic song, "Seek Ye First" was penned as a result of her experiencing a time of financial crisis, as she recounted. *"The Lord showed me through reading that Scripture that if I'd seek Him first then all these other things would be added to me. ..and He's really shown me He's faithful to that promise!"*

Later over many years, Karen served God faithfully in missionary ministry among the prostitutes and junkies of the red light districts of Amsterdam, Holland. *"My life had to be centred around the promises in God's Word and be living proof that a person can take God at His word. The lyrics of my songs, coupled with my simple melodies communicate these truths into the hearts of minds of those who listen!"*

Seek ye first the kingdom of God
And His righteousness,
And all these things shall be added unto you,
Hallelu, hallelujah!

Hallelujah! Hallelujah!
Hallelujah! Hallelu, hallelujah!

Man shall not live by bread alone,
But by every word
That proceeds from the mouth of God,
Hallelu, hallelujah!

Karen Lafferty (Copyright © 1972 Maranatha! Music/ Adm. by CopyCare, PO Box 77, Hailsham, BN27 3EF, England.) music@copycare.com / Used by permission

Someone To Care
Jimmie Davis

'Casting all your care upon him; for he careth for you!'
(1 Peter 5:7)

"My song, 'Someone To Care'", said Jimmie Davis (its writer), *"speaks of the Heavenly Friend of Sinners, the Great Someone who eternally cares for us all!...As human beings by nature, we easily become anxious. Our self-centeredness is often counterproductive worry because legitimate cares and concerns can be unloaded in every instance by prayer! The song reminds us that anxiety and prayer are two great opposing forces in Christian experience!"*
Jimmie knew that the antidote to worry (along with prayer and petition) is thanksgiving to the Great Someone who cares! Much of his songwriting career mirrored the mythical American dream with its "rags to riches" theme. He was literally a poor farm boy who rose to become the Governor of the State of Louisiana.

Jimmie Houston Davis was born on 11 September 1899 in a small, humble shotgun cabin nestled in the red clay hills of Beach Springs, Quitman, Louisiana. Today the cabin is a monument but once it was a home, a bare roof over three rooms housing a sharecropper, his wife, eleven children and assorted relatives! Studying at the Louisiana College in Pineville, Jimmie achieved a bachelor's degree despite, he claims, having only one shirt! *"I wore that little bitty shirt every day, washed it every night, and ironed it every morning!"* Musically inclined, Jimmie's sound in the Thirties and Forties wonderfully blended a form of crooning country music with a form of raw, blues-tinged Dixieland jazz. Singing became a passion for the hard-working Jimmie as he appeared on several local radio stations. RCA Records signed him up, which impressed Decca Records who signed him up in the mid-Thirties to a contract that lasted some forty years! In 1934 he recorded his standard entitled "Nobody's Darling But Mine" that was a hit for Frank Ifield in the UK in 1963. In 1938 Jimmie co-wrote "It Makes No Difference Now" that Bing Crosby charted a few years later. At that time in the Thirties, Jimmie was lured to the bright lights of the movies. He made regular appearances in small parts in the newly emerging talkies. *"But a big-time Hollywood career",* Jimmie admitted, *"never seemed to be my destiny. Returning to my beloved Louisiana, I started hitting big-time in country music before being bitten by the politics bug!"*

In 1938 he was elected Police Commissioner of Shreveport. He served for four years and was then elected to a six year term on the Louisiana Public Service Commission. He only served for two years, resigning to run for Governor. He had successful spells in the Governor's Office in the Forties and Sixties augmented by musical success. In 1939, Jimmie captured the imagination of the depression ridden world with a outstanding cheery song that became a favourite of millions. "You Are My Sunshine", his simple sing-along ditty soon became a standard, selling in its millions, making it one of the world's most popular melodies ever! In the years of World War II, the recorded versions of the song by Bing Crosby, Vera Lynn and Gene Autry were played on radio stations worldwide.

"In middle-age", Jimmy stated, *"I felt an inner call to write and sing gospel music!"* He faithfully fulfilled that new calling until the beginning of the new Century! Switching from country to gospel, he wrote many gospel songs. The best known of his gospel compositions were *"Someone to Care"* and *"Sheltered in The Hands Of God",* co-penned with Dottie Rambo. From middle age to old age, the Davis family resided in Baton Rouge, kept busy with a public relations business, music publishing and a farm (cattle and horse) managed by Jimmy Davis Junior.

Jimmie Davis, despite the successes, was not without his trials, his dear wife Alvern Adams died in 1967. *"With the divine aid of the Great Someone who cared"*, Jimmie said, *"I was given the strength to battle on! I found strength in weakness and joy in sadness!"*

Jimmie received the rare honour of being elected to both the *Country Music Hall of Fame* and the *Gospel Music Hall of Fame*. Even at the age of seventy-three he was still actively singing, recording and running again for the Governor's job for the third time! Assisting in his unsuccessful attempt was his new bride, Anna Gordon one of the original members of the Chuck Wagon Gang, a popular gospel group founded in 1936. Amazingly, Jimmie continued to sing right up to the start of the new millennium! Indeed, at the writing of this book in 2000 he was marking his 101st birthday with a song. Though not as mobile as in the past, he was still doing well. Then suddenly on Sunday 5 November 2000, he died. He left behind a greatly uplifting gospel music legacy.

But a certain Samaritan...had compassion on him...
and took care of him.
(Luke 10:33-34)

Suppertime
Ira Stanphill

*'Let us be glad and rejoice, and give honour to him:
for the marriage of the Lamb is come, and his wife hath
made herself ready.
And to her was granted that she should be arrayed in fine
linen, clean and white: for the fine linen is the
righteousness of saints.
And he saith unto me, Write, Blessed are they which are
called unto the marriage supper of the Lamb.'
(Revelation 19:7-9)*

Ira Stanphill wrote several beloved classics including "Mansion Over the Hilltop" (later recorded famously by Elvis Presley) , "Room At The Cross" (recorded by Kate Smith, Tennessee Ernie Ford, and the Statesmen), "Suppertime" (recorded by Ricky Van Shelton, Johnny Cash, Jimmie Davis, Faron Young, Vernon Oxford, and Jim Reeves) and "He Washed My Eyes With Tears" (recorded by Bev Shea). It is likely that these great recording artistes learnt many of their Stanphill songs from Blackwood Brothers' recordings.

Ira recounted how several years ago during a tent revival meeting in Germany conducted by the Assemblies of God evangelist-Willard Cantelone and soloist Al Garr, one of Ira's songs was sung in the German language. A local man entered the meeting secretly toting a gun planning apparently to commit suicide that evening. Instead, convicted, captivated and challenged by Ira's song and the sermon, the man went forward to the alter at the preacher's invitation surrendering to the claims of Christ on his life and was converted. Later the man became a minister of the gospel crediting Ira's song as being the catalyst that brought him to faith!

Born on 14 February 1914 in Bellview, New Mexico, Ira's parents homesteaded in the area following a harrowing covered wagon train journey from Arkansas. Then the family moved on to Coffeyville, Kansas. Later after Junior College, from 1930 to 1934 Ira sang on a daily radio programme on station KGGF. Two years later, he became an evangelist and then pastored churches in West Palm Beach, Florida and Lancaster, Pennsylvania. In 1966 he moved on to pastor the Rockwood Park Assembly of God Church in Fort Worth, Texas.

He wrote his first song at the age of seventeen, composing over 600 in his full life. From 1938 to 1967 he administrated his own publishing under the Hymntime banner before selling his rights to the Zondervan Publishing House.

"I knew Ira well!" James Blackwood recalled his dear, white-haired friend with heart-warming nostalgia. *"I had the wonderful privilege of doing some joint concerts with him. Hilton Griswold (our pianist from 1940-50) worked with his son (Larry), a pastor of a large church in Juliet, Illinois. Hilton syndicated a TV show to about twenty-five stations, taping the show in Chicago in Channel 38's Christian studio and later in Milwaukee. I guested several times with Ira. We also did some Sunday evening services.*

Ira and Gloria, his wife, were also with me on a Gaither Homecoming video taping in the early Nineties and we were booked for more. Sadly, he suffered a heart attack and died. But Gloria sang a song with me on the next video as a dear tribute to my brother in Christ! Several of Ira's songs were performed on that video taping day including, at my suggestion to Bill Gaither, 'Unworthy' by John McDuff of the McDuff Brothers. It was so moving. I had previously recorded the song on an RCA solo album."

Ira's song "Suppertime" speaks of the prophetic wedding supper of the Lamb. The imagery of a wedding to express the intimate relationship between God and His people has its roots in the prophetic literature of the Old Testament. A wedding supper was a joyous occasion, celebrated with music, feasting, drinking of wine, joking.

After the Exile from Egypt, written contracts were drawn up and sealed. The bridegroom went to the bride's home with friends and escorted her to his own house. Festive supper apparel was expected of guests and festivities lasted one or two weeks.

Separate processions for bride and groom were parts of the event where each was accompanied by musicians, dancers, torchbearers, well-wishers, and friends. Following the example of King Solomon, the bridegroom was crowned king of the festival and the bride also submitted to a ceremonial crowning. Traditionally, the feasting lasted for seven days. The profound truth of the union of Christ and his "bride," (the church) is beyond unaided human understanding.

Jesus saith unto them, Come and dine!
(John 21:12)

Surely Goodness And Mercy
Alfred B. Smith & John W. Peterson

> '*Surely goodness and mercy shall follow me all the days of my life: and I will dwell in the house of the LORD for ever.*'
> (Psalm 23:6)

Throughout the second half of the Twentieth Century, John W. Peterson was a prolific songwriter with thousands of gospel songs published as well as many sacred cantatas. One of his best known songs is the beloved "Surely Goodness and Mercy". Other favourites are "It Took A Miracle"(recorded by Eddy Arnold etc), "Shepherd of Love" (recorded by Bev Shea, Doug Oldham, etc), "Over The Sunset Mountains" (recorded by the Statler Brothers) and "Heaven Came Down"(recorded by Jimmie Davis, Kate Smith etc).

One of America's foremost contemporary composers, he was born on 1 November 1921 in the Swedish community of Lindsborg, Kansas, the youngest of seven children in a Swedish-American family. Sadly, his father died when he was four years old. He became a Christian at the age of twelve, and was greatly influenced in his Christian walk by his grandfather, Charles Nelson. Charles was the first to realise the outstanding creative gift that God had given his grandson and predicted that John would one day use that talent to the glory of God. John was an all-round musician playing piano and guitar as well as singing, writing his first song whilst still in High School. He sold his first composition in 1940 at the age of nineteen.

With the onslaught of hostilities, John was drafted and served in the United States Army Air Force as a pilot during World War II. Duty called and he was ordered upon to fly the dangerous lonely missions over the "China Hump" in the Himalayas. The exploits of these brave pilots on these hairy, desolate missions were lauded with the making of a John Wayne adventure movie at the time. In retrospect John Peterson says, *"Flying over those majestic peaks brought home to me the greatness and awesome character of God-the Good Shepherd who cares for His sheep! Those hazardous flights became the inspiration to many of my songs including 'Over The Sunset Mountains!'"*

Always keen to serve His Lord and Saviour, John's forthright Christian testimony earned him the nickname *Deacon* during his Air Force days. Every morning at his bunk bed, he would be mocked but secretly admired by his service buddies for reading his New Testament. After peace was finally declared, he went to the famed Moody Bible Institute and then entered the American Conservatory of Music in Chicago where he continued his musical education.

The co-writer, Alfred Barnerd Smith was born in Wortendyke in New Jersey on 8 November 1916. A boy prodigy on the violin, he guested as a soloist with the New York Symphony Orchestra under the baton of Walter Damrosch. Alfred studied at the Juilliard School of Music, the Moody Bible Institute and Wheaton College gaining a BA in 1943. His dormitory student room-mate was Billy Graham who as a fledgling evangelist used Alfred as his first song leader.

In 1941 Alfred began his first music publishing enterprise under the title of Singspiration. Sacred song compilation music books followed and in 1954 Alfred employed John Peterson as the music editor. Thus in 1955 he moved to Montrose, Pennsylvania to become editor-in-chief of Singspiration Inc, one of the largest gospel music publishing companies in America.

"Surely Goodness and Mercy" was written in 1958. One morning while he was tinkering on the piano improvising, waiting for a melody to take shape, his friend Alfred came in the room. Soon together, they fashioned the great song from the psalmist David's Shepherd Psalm. Eight years later, at the Greater London Billy Graham Crusade of 1966, the choir director-Cliff Barrows arranged it for Bev Shea and the mass choir. Instantly, "Surely Goodness and Mercy" became a crowd favourite.

John Peterson's association with Singspiration was a lengthy one. Ultimately, he rose to the executive editor position. He also continued to conduct as guest conductor at performances of his own numerous choral works in churches and auditoriums around the USA. His choral cantatas such as "Night of Miracles", "Easter Song" and others become firm favourites for over the decades among choirs all over the world, selling in their million of copies! Muriel Shepherd of the London Emmanuel Choir told me how "Night of Miracles" was a perennial Christmas favourite of hers and the Choir's vast audiences.

John Peterson and Alfred Smith's great song inspired by the last verse of King David's Shepherd Psalm, speaks confidently of the Good Shepherd's abiding "goodness and mercy" throughout life's pilgrimage. Both attributes of goodness and mercy refer to covenant benefits that personally follow the believer's lifestyle as they "dwell in the house of the Lord forever!" The word translated "follow" also means "pursue" in the original scriptures while "forever" is the Hebrew suggesting "throughout the years".

I am the Good Shepherd:
the Good Shepherd giveth His life for the sheep.
(John 10:11)

Sweet, Sweet Spirit
Doris Akers

'But be filled with the Spirit;
Speaking to yourselves in psalms and hymns and spiritual
songs, singing and making melody in your heart to the Lord;'
(Ephesians 5:18-19)

Just prior to her death, Doris Akers still displayed a great sense of humour. In the live "Homecoming" video taping of her song "Sweet, Sweet Spirit", she bravely pushed the host Bill Gaither from the piano stool, replacing him with herself. There amid light hearted banter, the mature lady showed Bill and the amused other Homecoming Friends how the song was intended to be sung. Throughout the years the song had received hundreds of interpretations ranging from Elvis Presley to Pat Boone.

The original melody and lyrics were written many years before by Doris following a moving experience during a pre-service prayer meeting with her Choir one special Sunday morning. She recalled, *"The Holy Spirit came down on me and my choir in a sweet gentle sense of powerful presence. I could see Him displayed on the choir members' warm expressions! I didn't know how the prayer meeting could conclude and wondered whether I should send word to the waiting pastor and congregation in the church sanctuary! Finally, I was compelled to tell the Choir that it was time to go!"*

From the experience was born a classic song, "Sweet, Sweet Spirit" from Doris' pen. It was first published in solo sheet-music form by Tim Spencer's Manna Music in 1965. Later that year it appeared in choral octavo form arranged by Kurt Kaiser. This became the accepted popular version of Doris' song. The melody was christened *Manna* (after the publishers- Manna Inc. - who were located in Burbank, California) by Tim Spencer's son Hal who was manager at the time.

For many years, Doris made her home in Columbus, Ohio although she was born on 21 May 1922 in Brookfield, Missouri, one of ten children. As a child she enjoyed music and poetry writing her first gospel song when she was merely ten years old. Despite her lack of any formal training, Doris learnt her skilful trade the hard way but, she said, the best way-by practical experience! For decades she successfully trained and directed choirs throughout the USA including famously the Skypilot Church Choir Of Los Angeles, California.

The Apostle Paul declared to the Ephesians, *"Do not get drunk...be filled with the Spirit!"* He used the Greek present tense to indicate that the filling of the Spirit is not a once-for-all experience. Repeatedly, as the occasion requires, the Holy Spirit empowers Christians for worship, service and testimony. Such a blessing is evidenced as Doris Akers' song says in faces and behaviour! The contrast between being filled with wine and filled with the Spirit is obvious. But there is something in common that enables the Apostle Paul to make the contrast, namely, that one can be under an influence that affects one, whether of wine or of the Spirit. When he spoke of being "filled with the Spirit" and when he speaks in Colossians of being "under the rule of the peace of Christ" and "indwelt by the word" of Christ, he means being under God's control! The effect of this control on believers is essentially the same in both passages: a happy, mutual encouragement to praise God and a healthy, mutual relationship with people. Every kind of appropriate song-whether psalms like those of the Old Testament, or hymns directed to God or to others (that Christians were accustomed to singing), could provide a means for praising and thanking God.

There's a sweet, sweet Spirit in this place,
And I know that it's the Spirit of the Lord.
There are sweet expressions on each face,
And I know that it's the presence of the Lord!
Sweet Holy Spirit, sweet Heavenly Dove,
Stay right here with us, Filling us with Your Love.
And for these blessings we lift our hearts in praise;
Without a doubt we'll know
That we have been revived,
When we shall leave this place.

The Night Watch
Cindy Walker

'I will lift up mine eyes unto the hills, from whence cometh my help.
My help cometh from the LORD, which made heaven and earth.
He will not suffer thy foot to be moved: he that keepeth thee will not slumber.
Behold, he that keepeth Israel shall neither slumber nor sleep.
The LORD is thy keeper: the LORD is thy shade upon thy right hand.
The sun shall not smite thee by day, nor the moon by night.
The LORD shall preserve thee from all evil: he shall preserve thy soul.
The LORD shall preserve thy going out and thy coming in from this time forth, and even for evermore.'
(Psalm 121:1-8)

Cindy Walker, the writer and composer of this beautiful gospel song (made famous by Jim Reeves, Paul Wheater and George Beverly Shea), was born in the Lone Star State of Texas, in the little town of Mart. From a very early age, the tender-hearted Cindy was surrounded by music. Her maternal Grandfather, F. L. Eiland was a hymnwriter whilst her mother Oree was an accomplished pianist.

Her songwriting career began at a very early age when she had a song recorded by the Paul Whiteman Orchestra, 'Casa De Manana' which she wrote for the Texas Centennial. But it was on the Californian west coast city of Los Angeles, in 1940 that her songwriting career really began in earnest.

Cindy's father, a cotton buyer, decided to leave Texas and head for Los Angeles to further his business. This move was a dream come true for Cindy as Los Angeles was considered the Mecca for popular music at that time. Cindy had her musical compositions with her in a small briefcase which she carried in the car on the tiresome journey. As the family searched the sun-drenched streets looking for a suitable apartment to rent they found themselves on the famous Sunset Boulevard in Hollywood. Suddenly, Cindy spied the Crosby Building and decided that the famous Bing Crosby would definitely be the right person to record her compositions! She persuaded the family to stop the car. With great audacity she marched boldly straight into his office complex. *'Oh, hi! My name's Cindy Walker! I'm a songwriter just up from Texas. I've got some great songs that I think'll be ideal for Mister Crosby to record!'* Initially nonplussed, the bemused secretary tried to tactfully dissuade Cindy from her endeavour. Not to be outsmarted, Cindy made her way into the inner office where an amused Larry Crosby consented to listen patiently to one of Cindy's crooning compositions, accompanied on the piano by her very star-struck mother!

Cindy created a good impression that day and so unbelievably, a prized appointment was made for Cindy to meet Bing Crosby himself at the Paramount Studios. It was the era of Hollywood's romance with the old west and western songs were in vogue. Bing was at the crest of his career-a superstar in movie circles- yet he sat submissively as this newcomer fresh from the heart of Texas sang a western song to him that she had just written entitled 'Lone Star Trail'. Clearly, Bing was suitably impressed and decided there and then that he would record it. *'My, my, my! You gotta a mighty pretty voice and that sure is a fine song there, Miss Cindy. I've some recording sessions comin' up and I've been kinda looking for a new cowboy song. That one of yours should suit me real well!'*

Accordingly, the wise and experienced 'ole groaner' (as he was affectionately known), recognised that Cindy was not only a quality songwriter but a gifted singing talent in her own right and persuaded her to follow a musical stage career in her own right. From this meeting, Cindy Walker went on to write hundreds of songs for many other famous artistes such as Jim Reeves, Roy Orbison, Dean Martin, Eddy Arnold, Ray Charles, Jack Greene, Merle Haggard and Bob Wills. The list is seemingly endless. She also appeared on the silver screen alongside such great celebrities as Gene Autry and Tex Ritter. Later, in the early Sixties, she starred with Redd Harper in the first Christian Western movie entitled 'Mister Texas' made by Worldwide Pictures part of the newly formed Billy Graham Association.

From her pen flowed many beautiful Christian songs that were recorded by the likes of George Beverly Shea and the Blackwood Brothers. Many of Cindy's popular songs such as 'Distant Drums', 'You Don't Know Me', 'Sugar Moon', 'Cherokee Maiden', 'Dream Baby' and 'Blue Canadian Rockies' went on to become Tin Pan Alley classics. She was honoured accordingly for her contributions to the music industry when she was inducted into the Country Music Hall of Fame in 1977.

Cindy's most famous sacred song-'The Night Watch'- was based on Psalm 121, a liturgical dialogue of confession and assurance. The key to the psalm's understanding is clear when seen as a pilgrimage song for pilgrims on the journey to Jerusalem. The trek to Jerusalem foreshadows the pilgrimage of life to the 'glory of heaven' into which the faithful will be received. Meanwhile, the psalm's key theme (occurring five times) is the Lord keeping the night watch, guarding over his people. The psalmist starts with his confession of trust in the Lord as he views the hills in the vicinity of Jerusalem, of which Mount Zion is one. Taken up with the greatness of his God, the psalmist addresses God as the Maker of heaven and earth, the one true God, the King of all creation. Then, like Cindy Walker's song, he expresses his assurance concerning the Unsleeping Guardian over Israel who keeps not only the day watch but the night watch too. He constantly watches over Israel, the One in whom the faithful may put unfaltering trust for unfailing protection in all of the changing seasons of life.

(We) who are kept by the power of God through faith
unto salvation ready to be revealed in the last time.
(1 Peter 1:5)

The Ninety And Nine
Elizabeth Clephane & Ira Sankey

'For the Son of man is come to save that which was lost.
How think ye? if a man have an hundred sheep,
and one of them be gone astray, doth he not leave the
ninety and nine, and goeth into the mountains, and seeketh
that which is gone astray?
And if so be that he find it, verily I say unto you, he
rejoiceth more of that sheep, than of the ninety and nine
which went not astray.
Even so it is not the will of your Father which is in heaven,
that one of these little ones should perish.'
(Matthew 18:11-14)

The bonnie land of Scotland bequeathed to the world a precious
treasure in this great hymn that Ira Sankey co-wrote and popularised.
The lyrics' writer, Elizabeth Clephane was born in 1830 and raised
in the beautiful countryside around Edinburgh. One of three sisters,
known as the delicate retiring member of the family, she was always
popular because of her helpful and happy nature. Cheerfully, she
served the poor and sick of her under-privileged community. In her
spare time she loved to write Christian poems.

Preacher, Dwight Moody and his soloist, Ira Sankey were riding
the train one cold, crisp morning from Glasgow to Edinburgh.
Stopping at a station for more passengers, Ira took the opportunity

to hop off the train to buy the morning newspaper from a platform newspaper stand. Back in his train seat, browsing through the pages of the paper, his eyes became transfixed on a new poem entitled 'The Ninety And Nine' by Elizabeth Clephane. Touched by the theme he clipped the section out and put it into his wallet.

That evening, Mr. Moody's exciting sermon was based on the Good Shepherd. The message over, with the audience spellbound, he turned to Ira for a suitable closing song. Pulling the newspaper clipping from his wallet, he placed it on his folding harmonium. Breathing a prayer, he struck up the chord of *A Flat* and began to sing. Divinely anointed, the tune came to him as he sang! Tears flowed freely from both Moody and Sankey and from many in the audience. It was the time for the evangelist to give the invitation to the lost sheep to return to the Great Shepherd of their souls.

The inspiring story of Elizabeth Clephane underlines what a comfort and joy gospel music can be! Ira believed passionately that whether in times of sunshine or in times of storm, gospel music can stir and inspire the Christian's spirit, and act as a "salt shaker" in society! Ira died at the dawn of the Twentieth Century, the greatest Victorian performing pioneer of inspirational music! Nowadays, many modern-day Christians don't realise that much of the gospel music we enjoy today comes to us because of the dedicated efforts of his ground-breaking enterprises. Yet it's sobering to realise that his fragile life was almost eliminated by a sniper's bullet in the American Civil War!

Ira David Sankey was born on 28 August 1840 ironically also in Edinburgh, but this time across the Atlantic in Pennsylvania. Raised on his father's farm, he worked there until his early teens. At the age of seventeen years, he moved to the peaceful neighbourhood of nearby Newcastle joining the Methodist Episcopal Church. Gifted with a fine voice and a charismatic disposition, he took part fully in the musical activities of the church, becoming Sunday School superintendent and leader of the choir. Rudely the tragic American Civil War interrupted these tranquil years.

He almost met his death by way of a Confederate sniper's bullet. At the end of his term as a Union soldier, he chose not to re-enter the army returning instead to peaceful Pennsylvania as a tax-man. Delighted to be back in his home church, soon his rich baritone voice began to attract attention. People would come from miles around just to hear his outstanding singing. Unknown to him during these years, he was unconsciously making preparation for his lifetime's work.

In 1870 at the age of 21, he suddenly met the challenge of a lifetime! Ira was appointed as a delegate to the Indianapolis *International Convention of the YMCA*. It was announced that an up and coming evangelist- preacher, Dwight L. Moody would lead a morning prayer meeting. On that day apparently Mr. Moody was not too enamoured with the quality of the singing and asked Ira to start something up when the next person stopped praying. This he did and when the evangelist heard his fine baritone voice, he immediately recognised the great gift Ira had been given by God.

Thus began a powerful partnership in conventions and missions that took Ira and Dwight all over the world. Ira would sing to thousands smartly dressed in his trendy, plush dress-suit. Then Dwight, the stocky, no-nonsense preacher would come to the platform and speak. Before long their influence ranged from the poorest of the poor right up America's President U.S. Grant and to the family of England's Royal Family. From the middle to end of the Nineteenth Century, the team of Moody and Sankey became increasingly well known worldwide! Their style of team evangelism pioneered the later work of Billy Graham, Cliff Barrows, and George Beverly Shea who became famous in the second half of the Twentieth Century!

There were ninety and nine that safely lay
In the shelter of the fold;
But one was out on the hills away,
Far off from the gates of gold-
Away on the mountains wild and bare,
Away from the tender Shepherd's care.

Lord, thou hast here Thy ninety and nine;
Are they not enough for Thee?
But the Shepherd made answer: This of mine

Has wandered away from Me;
And although the road be rough and steep,
I go to the desert to find My sheep.

But none of the ransomed ever knew
How deep were the waters crossed;
Nor how dark was the night that the Lord passed through,
Ere He found His sheep that was lost:
Out in the desert He heard its cry
Sick and helpless, and ready to die.

Lord, whence are those blood-drops all the way,
That mark out the mountain's track?
They were shed for one who had gone astray
Ere the Shepherd could bring him back.
Lord, whence are Thy hands so rent and torn?
They are pierced tonight by many a thorn.

But all through the mountains, thunder-riven,
And up from the rocky steep,
There arose a cry to the gates of heaven,
Rejoice! I have found My sheep
And the angels echoed around the throne,
Rejoice! for the Lord brings back His own!

Elizabeth Clephane & Ira Sankey

The Old Rugged Cross
George Bennard

'*But God forbid that I should glory,*
save in the cross of our Lord Jesus Christ,
by whom the world is crucified unto me, and I unto the
world.'
(Galatians 6:14)

George Bennard was born in 1873 in Youngstown, Ohio to a family of modest means. He lived to the goodly age of eighty-five years dying in Reed City, Michigan on 10 October 1958 bequeathing to the world a legacy of about 300 hymns and gospel songs. Coming to public fame during the campaigns of the animated evangelist-Billy Sunday, the most popular of George's compositions were "Speak My Lord!" and "The Old Rugged Cross".

Moving from Youngstown to Albia, Iowa and then to Lucas, Iowa, the family were initially unsettled. At sixteen, George lost his coal miner Father. The death forced on young George the burdensome strain of supporting his Mother and five brothers and sisters by him going down the coal pits. George was converted to Christ while still a youngster when he responded to the Gospel at a Salvation Army meeting. He received what he described as *"a call to the gospel ministry"* soon after his conversion but was hindered from higher education by financial restrictions. Undeterred, he diligently studied under the auspices of other local ministers and learned all that he required with hands-on experience and personal private study. Joining the Salvation Army, he served faithfully for many years in the leadership of a brigade before leaving to serve as an evangelist for the Methodist Episcopal Church in the USA and Canada. Following the death of his first wife, he married Hannah Dahlstrom.

He wrote over 300 gospel songs but "The Old Rugged Cross" became best known, described as America's most beloved hymn throughout the last Century. George Bennard stated that he recalled the circumstances surrounding the writing of this hymn in 1913. *"I was praying for a full understanding of the cross and its plan for Christianity. So I read and studied and prayed. The 'Old Rugged Cross' borne by Christ Jesus was humanly speaking a terrifying execution gallows, a disgrace to decent citizens. But in heaven's eyes, the 'Old Rugged Cross' represents Christ's glorious, vicarious death that gives mankind a new start!"* Thus, George explained how he felt that John 3:16 leapt from the printed page. He saw the Biblical use of the word "cross" embraced the two perspectives. Firstly, the wooden instrument of human torture and secondly, a symbolic representation of redemption. Our English word "cross" is derived from the Latin "crux". Crucifixion in Christ's time was one of the most cruel and barbarous forms of death known to man. It was practised, especially in times of war, by the Phoenicians, Carthaginians, Egyptians, and later by the Romans. So dreaded was it that even in the pre-Christian era, the cares and troubles of life were often compared to a cross. The agony of the crucified victim was caused by the painful but nonfatal character of the wounds inflicted. The abnormal position of a body on the cross meant that the slightest movement caused additional torture. Traumatic fever was induced by hanging for such a long time.

In New Testament, "the preaching of the Cross" is set forth as the "divine folly" (in sharp contrast to "earthly wisdom") when it is presented as God's medium of reconciliation and peace. It teaches that the penalties of the law were removed from the believer by the cross. To the Apostle Paul (as a Roman), the one crucified was an object of scorn, and (as a pious Hebrew) the one crucified was accursed. However, the Apostle said that he came to "glory in the cross", an absurdity of history were it not for the fact that the Apostle held the Crucified as the Christ of God!

While George watched the revelation unfold in the mind's eye of his understanding, with it came the theme and melody of "The Old Rugged Cross". *"Yet,"* he said, *"an inner voice seemed to clearly tell me to wait!...I was holding evangelistic meetings in Michigan so could not continue with the poem. A week later after a series of meetings in New York State I tried again to compose the poem but still could not! It was only after returning to Michigan for further evangelistic work that the floodgates loosed and opened! I was able to complete the poem with facility and despatch! A friend then aided me in putting it in manuscript form. Two years later, in 1915, it appeared in written form."*

What was the physical reason for Christ's death? Recent medical studies have sought an answer to the question. When a person is suspended by his two hands, the blood sinks rapidly into the lower extremities of the body. Within six to twelve minutes the blood pressure has dropped to half, while the rate of the pulse has doubled. The heart is deprived of blood, and fainting follows. Death during crucifixion is due to heart failure. Victims of crucifixion did not generally succumb for two or three days. Death was hastened by the breaking of the legs. But when they came to Jesus, eye witnesses said that they found that he was already dead so they did not break his legs. Among the Jews, a stupefying potion was prepared by the merciful women of Jerusalem, a drink that Christ refused. It was to such a death, the One who was coequal with God descended!

To commemorate the great hymnwriter, a memorial was erected where the students of Albion College (a well-established Methodist school institution in Albion), Ohio can daily ponder over "The Old Rugged Cross".

On a hill far away stood an old rugged cross,
The emblem of suffering and shame;
And I love that old cross where the dearest and best
For a world of lost sinners was slain.

So I'll cherish the old rugged cross,
'Til my trophies at last I lay down;

I will cling to the old rugged cross,
And exchange it some day for a crown.

There Is A Redeemer
Melody Green

'For I know that my redeemer liveth,
and that he shall stand at the latter day upon the earth.'
(Job 19:25)

The sun was shining when the telephone rang at the home of Melody Green on that fateful day in July 1982. The message of the call brought to Melody an acute, emotional storm to the otherwise peaceful day. On line was a familiar voice, a girl who worked in the offices of Last Days Ministries, the ministry that Melody and her husband Keith had started. In breathless and worried tones, the voice simply said, *"Our plane just went down! I'm going to call an ambulance, but I wanted to tell Keith first. Will you let him know?..."* *"Sure!..."* replied Melody instinctively. She found herself already slowly putting down the handset. But the sickening reality was that she knew that her husband already knew! Earlier that day after dinner, Melody had stood on her front porch waving off her husband and two of her three children (Josiah, aged three and Bethany, aged two) as they headed for the airstrip along with another family with six children. Neither they nor their pilot returned … Minutes later the call came. Pregnant, Melody found herself widowed with only one surviving child, Rebekah.

Meeting Keith in the Seventies, the happy hippie couple "had been and done everything" in their search for ultimate spiritual fulfilment. At last they found in Christ Jesus, the answers to their basic questions of life! Completely and radically changed by the new birth, the loving couple set out on their mission to save others especially from the wayward hippie community. Travelling, recording and ministering around the USA, Keith's message was one of "no compromise" as he battled against un-Godly standards. Together, Keith and Melody set up their Last Days Ministries, an evangelical organisation that also has a strong hand in pro-life campaigns, focusing on the anti-abortion stance.

In 1977 Melody wrote the modern hymn, *"There is a Redeemer."* When she played it to her husband Keith, his response was immediate. *"Honey, I just love it!...But I feel it's a little incomplete...Can I help you write a final verse?"* Melody nodded her consent as Keith seized pen and paper. Slowly, the lyrics of a final verse crystallised - *"When I stand in Glory, I will see His face! There I'll serve my King forever, in that Holy place!"* Those prophetic words from Keith were added to Melody's song in 1977 were peculiarly fulfilled in 1983. ·

The book of Job is renowned to be the oldest of all the Old Testament books. In it is found a surprising declaration from the suffering Job. *"I know that my Redeemer lives!"* This staunch confession of faith has since been appropriated by generations of Christians, especially through the medium of Handel's Messiah and songs such as *"There is a Redeemer"*. Although these songs celebrate man's redemption from guilt and judgement by Christ; Job had something else in mind! Although in other contexts, Job desired a Defender as an Advocate in heaven who would plead with God on his behalf, here the Redeemer seems to be none other than God himself! Job expressed his confidence that ultimately God would vindicate all his faithful servants in the face of all false accusations. In the end even after Job's life had ended, he was confident that his Redeemer would stand to defend and vindicate him! Job sensed that the ravages of his diseases would eventually bring about his death but that, nevertheless, he would "see God"! Of that he was absolutely certain! Death is not the end of existence! Someday every believer will stand in the presence of his/her Redeemer and (as Job said) see Him with his own eyes!

There is a Redeemer,
Jesus, God's own Son,
Precious Lamb of God,
Messiah, Holy One.

Thank You, O my Father,
For giving us Your Son,
And leaving Your Spirit—
Till the work on earth is done.

When I stand in glory
I will see His face,
And there I'll serve my King forever
In that holy place.

Turn Your Radio On
Albert Brumley

'They shall lift up their voice they shall sing for the majesty of the LORD, they shall cry aloud from the sea.
Wherefore glorify ye the LORD in the fires, even the name of the LORD God of Israel in the isles of the sea.
From the uttermost part of the earth have we heard songs, even glory to the righteous.'
(Isaiah 24:14-16)

Rural poet, Albert Edward Brumley was country-born on 29 October 1905 in Le Flore County, Oklahoma. His enterprising farming parents raised corn and cotton on their agrarian property. Always wild about "lyrics and music", in his teens he enthusiastically attended a community singing school in his home town of Rock Island, Oklahoma. His love for music deepened as he engaged himself in further study under the auspices of gospel music notables such as Virgil Stamps of the Stamps Quartet, Homer Rodeheaver (writer of "Then Jesus Came") and E.M. Bartlett (writer of "Victory In Jesus"). At the height of the Great Depression in 1931, he married "the love of his life", Goldie Edith Schell who he met in Powell, Missouri while teaching a singing school. Despite the economic struggles of the day, they parented five sons and one daughter. One son, Tom Brumley became a famed West Coast steel guitarist. He spent many successful years with country-hitmaker, Buck Owens as a member of his band, the Buckaroos.

Proud of her spouse's talent, Goldie Edith encouraged him to send his songs to a publisher. *"Honey, your songs are great! Any publisher -worth his salt- would agree with me and should publish them!"*

"Speaking of Albert E. Brumley", James Blackwood (of the Blackwood Brothers) remarked, *"I think one of the marks of a truly great man is humility and this is clearly evident whenever you met Albert E. Brumley. He was completely unassuming, always reluctant to be in the limelight. He was shy to receive the honours that he so bountifully deserved! Mr. Brumley was the second living man to be voted into the Gospel Music Hall of Fame, an honour definitely richly his due!"*

Albert died in 1977. His legacy is an opulent heritage of true classics from the Albert E. Brumley's pen including "I'll Fly Away", "River Of Memories", "I'll Meet You In The Morning", "Turn Your Radio On", "Jesus Hold My Hand" and many more. High-selling recordings of Brumley songs were plentiful throughout the last Century from the likes of Ray Stevens, the Statler Brothers, Pat Boone, Jim Reeves, Tennessee Ernie Ford and such. The Chuck Wagon Gang and the Statesmen devoted entire albums to Brumley material.

Singing always played a prominent part in the worship and national life of the ancient Hebrews and the early church. Throughout their history, it was not uncommon for the Jews to compose a song celebrating some special victory or religious experience such as the crossing of the Red Sea. The Psalter (or the Psalms) has been designated "The Song Book of Israel" and it contains many kinds of songs. The Apostle Paul urges all believers to sing. "Turn Your Radio On" encourages believers to tune into the songs of the saved.

The history of Hebrew music (as well as the history of Israel's higher civilisation in general and the organisation of the musical service in the temple) began with King David's reign. To King David has been ascribed not only the creation and singing of the psalms, but also the invention of musical instruments. During Solomon's reign, the number of Levites who were instructed in the songs of the

Lord was 288, divided into 24 classes. In Solomon's temple the choir formed a distinct body. They were furnished with homes and were on salary. Ezekiel says they had chambers between the walls and windows with southern views. The choir numbered 2,000 singers and was divided into two choirs.

Later, the orchestra and the choir personnel were greatly reduced in the second temple. The orchestra consisted of a minimum of two harps and a maximum of six; a minimum of nine lyres, maximum limitless; a minimum of two oboes and a maximum of twelve; and one cymbal. The second temple choir consisted of a minimum of twelve adult singers, maximum limitless. The singers, all male, were between 30 and 50 years of age. Five years of musical training was a prerequisite to membership in the second temple choir. In addition to the male adults, sons of the Levites were permitted to participate in the choir. God's people still sing as they have in every generation. The difference nowadays is, as "Turn Your Radio On" illustrates, the sound is broadcast widely on every modern form of media.

...as he came and drew nigh..
he heard music and dancing.
(Luke 15:25)

What Kind Of Love Is This?
Bryn & Sally Haworth

'*Behold, what manner of love the Father hath bestowed
upon us, that we should be called the sons of God:
therefore the world knoweth us not, because it knew him
not.
Beloved, now are we the sons of God,
and it doth not yet appear what we shall be:
but we know that, when he shall appear,
we shall be like him; for we shall see him as he is.*'
(1 John 3:1-2)

The writer of "What Kind Of Love Is This?"- Bryn Haworth says, *"The Bible gives rise to the unique revelation that God in His very nature and essence is love! Indeed, God not only loves, He is love! In this supreme attribute all the other attributes are harmonised. His own Son, Jesus Christ, is the unique object of this eternal love. We know that God loves the world as a whole, but also individual, sinners and especially believers in Christ! It's exciting to realise that Love is the very nature of God and the greatest of all Christian virtues! Love is essential to man's relations to God and his fellowman. Christ said that on love hangs all the law and the prophets, it is the fulfilment of the law. Love found its supreme expression in the gift of God in His Son's self-sacrifice on Calvary!"* Slimly built, Bryn Haworth was born in 1948 in Darwin, Lancashire. His love affair with his chosen musical instrument, the guitar, began when he received the gift of a classical guitar at the age of eleven. He took classical guitar lessons for a year, but his great yearning was to learn to play electric guitar, just like his heroes The Shadows (Sir Cliff Richard's legendary musical group). Bryn's obvious talent for this instrument led to him playing professionally at the age of sixteen leading to tours with several acts including Sir Cliff Richard (in Australia and New Zealand). The special Haworth talents became in great demand in session musician work. All this time, he was writing his own pop songs for his own albums. He states, *"I tend to write a whole load of songs at one time then select and retain the best ones!"*

Bryn's musical career was greatly influenced by "rhythm and blues" music. *"When I went to America, I found myself playing with Little Feat's drummer, Richie Hayward and expatriate Liverpool singer, Jackie Lomax. Back in Britain, I worked with Pete Wingfield, Rosko Gee, Alan Spenner and Bruce Rowland."* Bryn became well respected among these "musicians' musicians". Indeed, his musical ability was called into use on Joan Armatrading's outstanding album. He was responsible for the brief but extrodinaryily eloquent slide-guitar solo, "Like Fire" as well as playing mandolin on another song.

He became recognised as a remarkable exponent of the slide (or bottleneck) guitar, a technique derived from the blues and such greats as Eric Clapton, Muddy Waters, Duane Allman. Bryn's sound though created a gentler approach which whilst complementing his own songs, also created a sound like nobody else. This blend of Afro-American forms plus his own unique sounds produced something that became unique to Bryn.

Bryn tells me that he was not bought up in a Christian home and had no interest in Christianity in his early years. Then things as he recalled changed. *"Before I became a Christian, I started to believe there was a God. For three years I wondered how I could get to know Him! Then one day I was passing a big circus tent. On the notice outside it said, 'I Am The Way The Truth and the Life'. So I thought, 'Right, I'll go in!' which I did! The evangelist , Dick Saunders was preaching that day and he clearly pointed out that Jesus was the true way to God. And so right there and then I asked Him into my life!"*

As the years followed, Bryn and his wife Sally, worked closely together, travelling to numerous concerts all over Great Britain and elsewhere. Going to any Bryn Haworth concert meant that audiences would be professionally "entertained" firstly by great guitar music along with sounds from numerous other stringed instruments, all played in the unique "Haworth style". Audiences also found great laughter at this man's gentle sense of humour. But more importantly, the listener was blessed by his powerful testimony to the Lord's Grace in his life. His song "What Kind of Love Is This?" reflects the wonder and awe that Bryn feels when confronted by the fact that the great Lord of Heaven, Jesus Christ, should give His life for guilty people such as he. *"Christ died that we might know for ourselves personally, the love of this great God as individuals."*

What kind of love is this?
That gave itself for me
I am the guilty one
Yet I go free.
What kind of love is this?
A love I've never known
I didn't even know His name,
What kind of love is this?

By grace I have been saved,
it is the gift of God.
He destined me to be His son,
Such is His love.
No eye has ever seen,
No ear has ever heard,
Nor has the heart of man conceived,
What kind of love is this?

Where No One Stands Alone
Mosie Lister

'Hide not thy face far from me;
put not thy servant away in anger:
thou hast been my help;
leave me not, neither forsake me, O God of my salvation.
When my father and my mother forsake me, then the LORD
will take me up.'
(Psalm 27:9-10)

Mosie Lister remains one of the greatest and most enduring of the Southern gospel tunesmiths of the last Century. More than 500 songs have flowed from his artistic pen. For many years, Mosie served as the active choir director of the Riverside Baptist Church in sunny Tampa, Florida, the town of his residence.

Born in 1921 in Cochran, Georgia where his dear father was a singing teacher and choir director, his first ambitious song was published at the age of eighteen years. He gained a taste for the discipline and fulfilment of songwriting, pitching his compositions to the Atlanta gospel groups of the late Forties. Soon after this , he gained considerable radio experience. His elementary and secondary education qualifications were gained in Middle Georgia College where he majored in Harmony and Counterpoint and arrangements for piano and organ. By 1948, he was ready to perform gospel music on the road in churches, theatres and schools. Originally part of an early Statesmen Quartet line up, he decided, after great prayer and deliberation, to quit and concentrate on songwriting instead forming the Mosie Lister Publications in1953. Following national service, Mosie was further encouraged by his dear wife to compose more seriously.

"Looking back", he declared, *"I have written so many songs that even I have lost count!"*

Outstanding quality songs of Lister vintage include "How Long Has It Been", "Where No-one Stands Alone", "Then I Met The Master" and "Til The Storm Passes By". "His Hand In Mine" is perhaps Mosie Lister's greatest! When this worthy songwriter was proudly inducted into the rare honour of the *Gospel Music Hall of Fame* in 1998, the playing of the recorded version by the Blackwood Brothers' "His Hand In Mine" formed part of the induction ceremony. It became the classic title-song of Elvis Presley's first gospel album for RCA recorded at the height of his high-flying career. Artistes who have recorded Lister materials through the years are legion but include BJ Thomas, Jim Reeves, Elvis Presley, Faron Young, Jan Howard, Jimmie Davis, Jimmy Dean, Webb Pierce, and Bev Shea. In the late Nineties, he resided in Tampa, Florida. Even in old age, he still produced quality material and was a frequent guest on the Gaither Homecoming videos of the Nineties.

In 1955, Mosie was driving lazily down a north Georgia highway. Alone, he was gently humming to himself in tempo with the rhythm of the car as he often did. Then suddenly, inspired words and music bubbled forth as the chorus of "Where No One Stands Alone" took shape. A year later, he wrote the verses inspired by the Psalmist David's words recorded in Psalm 27:9-10. Imagining himself in David's shoes, Mosie recalled the product of his meditation. *"Placing myself in David's frame of mind, the words to the verses of 'Where No One Stands Alone' came easily!"*

A few years later, he received a phone call from an acquaintance in New York City. "Hey, Mosie have you thought about writing a song for Mahalia Jackson?...She is such a quality singer, man!" Mosie's creativity was challenged. He had heard and seen on the news bulletins how Mahalia's popularity was increasing in the times of building tensions nationally over the civil rights issues. He brought the matter before the Lord in prayer and felt that God did want him to say something prophetic in a song. The result was the birth of the song-"Til The Storm Passes By". Ironically, Mosie never managed to get Mahalia to record the song but hundreds of other vocalists did and it became a blessing to millions firstly, in the USA during the difficult days of social division and civic unrest! Secondly, the song became a blessing overseas even in countries as far away as New Guinea.

Once I stood in the night with my head bowed low
In the darkness as black as could be,
Then my heart felt alone and I cried, O Lord
Don't hide your face from me.
Hold my hand, all the way every hour every day
From here to the great unknown!
Take my hand, let me stand,
Where no one stands alone!

Wonderful Grace
John Pantry

'But God, who is rich in mercy, for his great love wherewith he loved us,
Even when we were dead in sins, hath quickened us together with Christ, (by grace ye are saved;)
And hath raised us up together,
and made us sit together in heavenly places in Christ Jesus:
That in the ages to come he might show
the exceeding riches of his grace in his kindness toward us through Christ Jesus.
For by grace are ye saved through faith;
and that not of yourselves: it is the gift of God:
Not of works, lest any man should boast.'
(Ephesians 2:4-9)

John Pantry says, *"The Apostle Paul's words in Ephesians 2:4-9 are important for understanding God's wonderful grace otherwise described as His kindness, unmerited favour and forgiving love! Paul said believers have been saved!... 'Saved' has a wide range of meanings that includes salvation from God's wrath that we've all incurred by our sinfulness. The tense of the verb suggests a completed action with emphasis on its present effect! Paul's words confirmed the necessity of 'faith in Christ' as the only means of being made right with God. No human effort can contribute to our salvation; it is the gift of God. One cannot earn salvation by observing religious law! Such a legalistic approach to salvation is consistently condemned in Scripture. No one can take credit for his or her salvation!"*

Singer/songwriter, John Pantry has a varied career structure ranging from record producer to radio DJ. Born in Harrow, Middlesex, just north of London, he developed an early interest in music as a member of his local church choir. He recalls with a smile, *"They tried to get me to learn to read music! But like most other kids, I didn't try very hard at it, something I was to regret afterwards! But, nevertheless, later in life, I taught myself to read music!"*

After leaving school, John decided that he would like to get into the UK's booming recording business of the Sixties. Fortunately, he became a trainee to the internationally respected IBC Studios in central London's Portland Place where he trained for two and a half years.

Soon he was engineering on albums for an impressive array of musicians such as the Bee Gees, Small Faces, Kinks and Manfred Mann. Alongside his obvious engineering and recording talent, he was also becoming recognised as a very proficient songwriter. Whilst he was working in the studios, John recorded a few demo discs of his compositions. Soon he was having singles recorded by several household names of the time including Billy J. Kramer and the Fortunes.

John then recorded his own single-the James Taylor song-"Something In The Way She Moves" that became a hit in the USA. He then won a recording contract with Phillips Records who released his first album appropriately entitled "John Pantry" in 1973. Unfortunately, the success he felt that he deserved did not materialise. John also ran his own company that made TV advertising jingles for various products.

Once again he began writing and producing for other artistes. Among these assignments was a Christian group called Parchment whose inspiring "Light Up The Fire" song (which John produced) seemed to capture the savour of the British Christian scene of that time. Through his increasing contact with Christian musicians, John was led into a personal relationship with Jesus Christ. This in turn bought him into contact with Christian artistes who wanted him to produce their albums such as Adrian Snell, Graham Kendrick, Dave Pope and many others.

John remembers, *"When I became a Christian, it seemed that a high proportion of my secular work just seemed to fold up! It wasn't that I stopped taking that kind of business, its just that the phones stopped ringing as far as those clients were concerned."* It was a very difficult time for him and a situation he found hard to understand. Suddenly, he was finding that he needed to rely on what he called his Christian work to survive! Work in Christian music in the UK at that time was extremely difficult to procure. Looking back, John says that he realised that God did know best because as a "baby Christian", he would not have been able to resist the un-Christian influences that the world had to offer. Later when stronger in the faith, John was able to resume his secular work.

In Seventies, John became a director of "Ears and Eyes" a Christian record production company with fellow directors Kevin Hoy and New Zealander, Chris Norton. There followed numerous record productions plus a year in California producing albums for Maranatha Music before he produced his first solo Christian album- "Empty Handed"- on the UK's Kingsway label in 1978.

Returning from the USA, John settled in the country environs of Essex on the English east coast with his wife Jackie and their three children. In 1989 John began studying to become an Anglican minister and was ordained accordingly. He also worked for the Scripture Union organisation as a preacher, running seminars, workshops and missions to churches, schools and prisons, as well as performing at his own gospel concerts.

Wonderful grace that gives what I don't deserve
And pays me what Christ has earned
Then lets me go free
Wonderful grace that gives me the time to change
Washes away the stains that once covered me

And all that I have
I lay at the feet
Of the Wonderful Saviour who loves me

You Laid Aside Your Majesty
Noel Richards

Let this mind be in you, which was also in Christ Jesus:
Who, being in the form of God, thought it not robbery to be
equal with God:
But made himself of no reputation,
and took upon him the form of a servant,
and was made in the likeness of men:
And being found in fashion as a man, he humbled himself,
and became obedient unto death, even the death of the cross.
(Philippians 2:5-8)

Inspired by Philippians 2:5-8, Noel Richards' song "You Laid Aside Your Majesty" represents the cream of this worship troubadour's songwriting and performing ability. It speaks of Christ's humiliation and exaltation. Affirming that Jesus is fully God, yet the song states that His status and privileges were not things He forcibly retained. Christ emptied Himself, not by giving up deity, but by laying aside His majesty, submitting to the humiliation of becoming a man. Consequently, God's design was that all people everywhere should worship and serve Jesus as Lord. Ultimately all will acknowledge him as Lord, whether willingly or not.

Noel's albums formed the foundation of his well-deserved aspiring career in Christian music during the Nineties. Since 1986, Noel recorded many albums and featured on scores of "live" recordings from various major events. He and his wife, Tricia's worship songs are nowadays used in thousands of churches around the world and they have travelled to more than 25 countries and to every continent. Surprisingly he is not the author of all his album songs! When he writes songs such as "There Is Power In The Name of Jesus", "To Be In Your Presence", "All Heaven Declares", "You Laid Aside Your Majesty" and "By Your Side", it's a wonder why one has to dip into other peoples' repertoire!

Noel's childhood was spent in the Land of Song (Llantrisant near Cardiff, Wales) where he attended the local, lively Pentecostal church. Around the age of eight or nine years old, he became a Christian but made a more definite re-commitment at the age of fifteen. This decision coincided with the advent of a new church minister, John Glass, fresh out of Bible college. He was in his early twenties and became a role model to Noel. He really took an active role in discipling him. Also, being a guitarist himself, he began to teach Noel to play, sing and present himself publicly. John acquainted Noel with the swelling contemporary Christian music scene in the UK. This was 1971 and the early days of visionary organisations that gave birth to music ministries. The first big Christian concert that Noel ever attended was at the Colston Hall in Bristol where Pete Meadows hosted an 'It's Buzz!' event. One of the artistes paraded was a young aspiring Graham Kendrick. As Noel watched him perform, he thought to himself , *"This is what I want to do!"* God planted a seed of hope in his life at that juncture. The earliest of his singing opportunities came through his home church and his travel with preacher- John and others when they ministered in other churches. On one occasion, John introduced him to his associate who was organising the Youth for Christ set-up in Bristol. Soon Noel became involved with schools evangelism and eventually entered into full time Christian work.

Initially on leaving school, Noel worked in a drawing office for three years but found it incredibly boring! He then progressed to something marginally more interesting, selling toiletry products to supermarkets. However, all his excess time was consumed doing concerts. His day job was simply a way of making ends meet. When he was summoned to work full time with Youth for Christ, he went for it with great enthusiasm!

"I spent a year on the road going from mission to mission, event to event, on a very steep learning curve! But overall it was a good time! I had to learn a lot and did a lot of growing up. I'm grateful to the people who had input into my life at that stage. YFC leader, Clive Calver in particular was a great encourager!" The songs Noel wrote in those days tended to be evangelistic, mainly majoring on the Gospel message. He never dreamed that he could write worship songs that churches worldwide could sing. He laughingly remembers, *"As it seemed that most of the songs used in church worship were written by Charles Wesley and such, I genuinely believed that you had to be dead to be a hymnwriter!...Written in 1979, the first of my songs published was 'Lord and Father, King for ever'."*

Noel met his dear wife to be, Tricia on his very first schools' mission in Plymouth in 1975 while working with Phil Vogel (National Director of Youth for Christ). Tricia was one of the senior girls at the first school he visited and was sent out to meet him. She stood outside the school with a friend who was not a Christian. As Noel walked across the car park, she said something very strange to her friend, *"You see that guy there! I'm going to marry him!"*

"She had never met me", says Noel, *"but obviously her prophetic gifting was in operation! Three years later in September 1978, we were married, going on to parent two children, Sam and Amy!"* Noel and Tricia resided in Plymouth until 1980. Amid demanding pressures, their local church grew quickly but they felt themselves that they and others in leadership were young and inexperienced. Their Church had only one senior leader and eventually the workload proved too great. Another church leader, Gerald Coates (from Cobham, Surrey) came to their church several times to speak and it was to him that they turned for advice. He suggested that the senior leader should take a sabbatical. *"Why don't you let him come to Cobham for a couple of years?"* Gerald said. *"Let the others continue to lead the church in Plymouth and we can support and help them!"* Everyone, however, liked the idea of the senior leader's move but they also wanted to remain a community too and be committed to staying together. *"If one goes, we all go!"* was their response. Suddenly, Gerald had the senior leader, the leadership team and congregation all expressing a desire to move to Cobham, a small

town just outside the London area. The result was that they closed
the Plymouth church and fifty people moved to Cobham, 200 miles
away!

Hence, Noel, Tricia and the others became part of Cobham
Christian Fellowship (now Pioneer People), led by Gerald. *"Imagine
the shock"*, says Noel, *"of telling the Cobham Fellowship that they
were about to be invaded by about fifty people from the other end of
the country! They were around 200 people then, so it was quite a
large extra number to absorb! Cobham remains our home base, after
all those years. I have led the worship team there from 1991 until
1996 and still regularly lead the church in worship. I've worked on
a full-time basis with Gerald Coates, from 1983 until the present
time!"*

In 1997, Noel and Gerald Coates organised and hosted "Champion
of the World" at London's Wembley Stadium. Almost 45,000 people
attended, the biggest contemporary worship event ever staged in the
UK. Their vision is to "summon the youth of the world and the young
at heart" to worship! As the new millennium dawned, it hailed Noel
Richards as one of Britain's leading contemporary Christian
songwriters.

You laid aside Your Majesty,
Gave up everything for me,
Suffered at the hands of those You had created.
You took all my guilt and shame,
When You died and rose again;
Now today You reign,
In heaven and earth exalted.

I really want to worship You, my Lord,
You have won my heart
And I am Yours for ever and ever;
I will love You.
You are the only one who died for me,
Gave Your life to set me free,
So I lift my voice to You in adoration.

Alphabetical Hymn/Songwriter Index

Scripture Index

Matthew 18:20/As We Are Gathered
Matthew 21:5-11/Meekness And Majesty
John 3:5-7/Born Again
John 14:19/Because He Lives
John 11:25/He's Alive!
John 12:32/I Saw A Man
John 20:14-16/In The Garden
Romans 8:15/Abba Father
Romans 8:28-29/Jesus You Are Changing Me
Romans 15:13/Jesus You're The Joy Of Living
Galatians 4:6-7/Father God I Wonder
Galatians 6:14/The Old Rugged Cross
Ephesians 2:4-9/Wonderful Grace
Ephesians 5:18-19/Sweet, Sweet Spirit
Philippians1:6/ He's Still Working On Me
Philippians 2:5-8/You Laid Aside Your Majesty
Philippians 2:9/For His Name Is Exalted
Philippians 3:7-9/He's Everything To Me
Colossians 2:2-3/Blessed Assurance
1 Thessalonians 4:17-18/God Be With You Till We Meet Again
1 Peter 1:18/I Am Redeemed
1 Peter 2:6-7/ I'd Rather Have Jesus
1 Peter 5:7/Someone To Care
1 John 3:1-2/What Kind Of Love Is This?
1 John 4:10/How I Love Thee
Revelation 1:17-18/At Your Feet We Fall
Revelation 19:7-9/Suppertime